California
Winery Tours

Automobile Club of Southern California

Cover photo—James Blank
©Richard Gillette

Writer, Nadja Djekich • **Graphic Artist,** Michael C. Lee

Editor, Kristine Miller • **Editorial Assistant,** Patricia Vaquero

---

Although information presented in this publication has been carefully researched and was as accurate as possible at press time, the Automobile Club of Southern California is not responsible for any changes or errors which may occur. When practical, it is wise to verify information immediately prior to your visit.

Only attractions or establishments that are approved by an Automobile Club of Southern California field representative may advertise. The purchase of advertising, however, has no effect on inspections and evaluations. Advertisements provide readers with additional information that may be useful in selecting what to see and where to stay.

Additional advertisements (excluding attractions and establishments) for travel-related services may also be included in ACSC publications. Acceptance of these advertisements does not imply endorsement by ACSC.

ISBN: 1-56413-241-2
Printed in the United States of America

Copyright © 1995 by Automobile Club of Southern California
Travel Publications Department
2601 South Figueroa Street, Los Angeles, California 90007

Contents

Cities: Escondido, Fontana, Guasti-Ontario, Julian, Los Angeles, Mira Loma, Ontario, Rancho Cucamonga, San Diego and Temecula.

Cities: Arroyo Grande, Buellton, Creston, Harmony, Lompoc, Los Olivos, Nipomo, Oak View, Paso Robles, San Luis Obispo, San Miguel, Santa Barbara, Santa Maria, Santa Ynez, Solvang, Templeton and Ventura.

Introduction

Why tour a winery? Winemaking is a family endeavor. Although multinational conglomerates may own a few of the famous-name wineries, often—in the case of Mondavi, for instance, or Gallo—the wineries are still operated by the founders or their families. Visit a winery and you will often come face to face with California history across the tasting bar or in the cellars and caves. Immigrant Europeans of the 19th century saw images of their homeland etched into the state's coastal valleys. The Beringer family went so far as to build a replica of their Bavarian home on the hillsides of St. Helena. In addition to the landscape that resembled parts of Italy, France and Germany, California's Mediterranean climate proved conducive to grape-growing. California has more than 800 wineries, with over half of them in the Russian River and Napa-Sonoma areas. If you screen out the modern tourist-oriented trappings of today's Napa Valley—where traffic is heavy even on a rain-swept winter weekend—you may gain a glimpse of Bordeaux, Tuscany or Alsace.

This book describes many California wineries offering tours to individuals and small groups. Some wineries, such as Beringer and Mondavi, take groups on rehearsed, timed tours. Others, such as Arciero and St. Supéry, provide well-marked, informative self-guided tours. And at a few, such as Storrs Winery, Black Sheep Vintners and Caparone, the tasting room and winery are housed in the same building: no trying to keep up with the group as it descends into dark, humid caves or walking down aisles of tanks in hangar-sized storage areas. Fetzer, in Hopland, has a spectacular organic vegetable garden; Ferrari-Carano, Peju Province and Justin Vineyards have lovely flower gardens; Deer Park Escondido, Perry Creek and Arciero exhibit classic automobiles and race cars; the Hess Collection and Clos Pegase house their owners' art collections and double as private art museums. Many have reserved an area to display the art work of local artists.

If tours are given by appointment, be sure to call or write the winery at least a week ahead of your intended visit. *Even if no appointment is required, it is advisable to call the wineries on your itinerary in advance.* Special events can change regular schedules. Some wineries use their facilities for weddings or other private events that preclude uninvited visitors; public concerts, festivals or special tastings may cause traffic delays and parking difficulties. Arrangements should always be made in advance for group visits; many wineries will schedule private tours and tastings for large parties. There are also some wineries that are not located at the vineyard address; for this reason it is best to verify their location ahead of time. It is also plausible that wineries change ownership; sometimes they close for a time before reopening and other times they may not be open to the public.

The fall harvest is the busiest time of year, so September and October provide the best opportunity to see the full range of winemaking operations. Many of the smaller wineries cannot accommodate visitors at this time, however, because staff members cannot take time away from their other duties. Winter, the quietest season, is a good time to avoid crowds. Activity gradually resumes in spring and summer, when the vineyards need tending and the tourist season gets under way.

Besides touring the winery itself, visitors can learn about the effects of various winemaking techniques through tasting. Tasting and drinking are two different activities, and some wineries charge a nominal fee for tasting to discourage those hoping for a free before-dinner drink. Tastings, or "sensory evaluations," are really just a specialized version of "show-and-tell." Tasting room staff members are educators, not bartenders, and often can provide a wealth of information not only about the wines they pour, but about the background of the winery, local history and many other subjects. How does the color and taste differ between a Cabernet, Zinfandel, Pinot Noir and Merlot? How does Chardonnay taste when it has been fermented in stainless steel instead of oak? How do grapes grown on the valley floor differ from those grown on a steep mountainside?

How should you transport the wine you purchase during your travels? The best solution usually is to have the winery ship it to your home, but wine can only be shipped to states that have reciprocal trade agreements with California: Colorado, Idaho, Illinois, Missouri, New Mexico, Oregon, Washington and Wisconsin. If you want to transport the wine yourself, store the wine in the coolest part of your car, out of direct sunlight and on its side. Adequate padding will prevent bottle breakage; make sure bottles and wine glasses are positioned so they won't bounce against hard surfaces. Styrofoam wine shippers for single and double bottles are ideal and can be purchased at many mailing outlets. When you arrive home, let the bottle sit a day or two before opening.

Wine may taste a bit "off" if opened immediately after a rough journey or cross-country shipping—this is referred to as "bottle sickness."

Many travelers plan to visit several wineries in a day's journey. It's a good idea to eat a hearty meal before setting out, or to plan a picnic at one of the wineries with facilities. If a winery has a deli, cafe or refrigerated items for sale, it will be noted in the listing, as well as picnic facilities. Keep in mind that food and fuel are

found primarily in downtown areas or along major highways.

Winemaking is primarily an agricultural endeavor, and towns are sometimes separated by miles of vineyards and not much else. To help you locate wineries in the same vicinity, this book is divided into five major geographic regions: Southern California; Central Coast; Monterey to San Francisco Bay; Napa, Sonoma, Mendocino and Lake region; and the Central Valley and Sierra Foothills region. Wineries are listed alphabetically within each section. This book also contains regional maps showing winery locations.

Showing the Way

Several publications of the Automobile Club of Southern California and the California State Automobile Association cover these areas in varying amounts of detail. ACSC's *Central and Southern Camping* and *Northern Camping* maps provide information on public and selected private campgrounds throughout California. For the southern part of the state, county maps show primary and secondary highways, city maps provide complete street coverage for the more developed and congested areas, and a *Southern California Bed and Breakfast* book lists unique places to stay the night. These and many other ACSC publications are sold to the public at selected retail outlets throughout Southern California and are available to AAA members at ACSC and CSAA offices. Other AAA and CSAA publications offered exclusively to AAA members can be obtained at ACSC and CSAA offices. (For more information on AAA membership, call your nearest AAA affiliated office.)

California Wine History

California's original winemakers were Spanish missionaries led by Father Junípero Serra. Between 1769 and 1823, as they moved north from Baja California founding their chain of 21 missions, they also planted a succession of vineyards. From what became known as the Mission grape, the Franciscans produced a wine that was adequate for sacramental, medicinal and table use.

For nearly 60 years, the missionaries were California's only viticulturists. In the 1820s, commercial wine growing was launched in the Los Angeles area. Joseph Chapman, the first commercial grower, was followed a decade later by Jean Louis Vignes, a Frenchman who brought vine cuttings with him from Europe. Soon these pioneers had competitors. The Gold Rush brought an increased demand for wine, and with it an influx of European winemakers. Krug, Mirassou, Korbel, Beringer, Martini and Concannon—the mixed heritage of California's wine industry is reflected in the names of its founders.

Among the immigrant viticulturists was a Hungarian named Agoston Haraszthy. Like Jean Louis Vignes, he brought European grape varieties to Southern California. In 1857 he moved to Sonoma, where his vinifera vines thrived. Subsequently, Haraszthy was commissioned by the state's governor, John G. Downey, to tour Europe and return with reports of winegrape cultivation and winemaking practices there. When he returned home, he brought more cuttings from the vineyards of Europe. His work, along with that of families such as Mirassou, fostered the conversion of California vineyards from the Mission grape to premium Old World varieties such as Cabernet Sauvignon and Chardonnay.

California's progress was almost completely reversed by a dreaded plant louse, phylloxera. This pest was discovered in England in 1863; by the end of the century it had virtually destroyed the vineyards of France and caused widespread damage in other European countries. California got its first hint of danger in 1874, when a vineyard in Sonoma County was found to be afflicted by the pest. Soon phylloxera was devastating the vines of Sonoma, Napa, Yolo, El Dorado and Placer counties. Finally a remedy was discovered. By grafting the fragile European grapevines to sturdier American rootstock, the vineyards could be saved. It meant replanting nearly every vineyard, both in America and Europe, but it salvaged the wine industry. Paso Robles and Amador County are two areas that were never afflicted by the louse, and some very old pre-phylloxera vines still survive there.

Not long after California's vineyards recovered from phylloxera, Prohibition dealt its blow. A few wineries were able to survive by producing medicinal and sacramental wines, but most went out of business. Grape growers fared better—because home winemakers were allowed to produce 200 gallons annually, there was still a strong market for grapes.

After 13 years Prohibition was finally repealed, but the industry's troubles were not over. The sudden demand for wine could not be met—except, in part, with inferior or even synthetic wines. California winemakers were in danger of losing their market as well as their reputation. As a means of self-protection they founded the Wine Institute, which in turn convinced the government to establish quality and labeling standards for wines sold in the United States.

At last the wine industry was back on its feet. The quality of California wines, as well as the demand for them, was higher than ever before. Despite two wine depressions, California winemaking experienced steady overall growth from the 1930s to the 1960s. Since then, the industry has fared even better thanks to a rapidly expanding market.

Large corporations have enjoyed a substantial share of the wine boom. Of the 20 largest wineries in the United States, 18 are located in California. The largest, E & J Gallo, produces four times as much wine as any other corporation in the United States. Corporate names are behind some of the more widely distributed labels, including Fetzer, Beaulieu, and Beringer. Although the benefits of corporate control are widely debated, the big companies have helped meet the demand for inexpensive table wines.

Small, premium wineries—those concentrating on a few varietal wines produced in limited quantity—have also prospered; their number increases each year. Many have won international recognition in prestigious tastings and competitions.

There were predictions that California's wine industry would reach its peak in the mid-1970s. Instead, it continued to expand. Advances in winemaking techniques and the increasing quality of California fruit attracted international attention and a vast amount of foreign investment during the 1980s. Many prominent wineries are now owned by French, German, Japanese, British, Swiss and Spanish concerns, and in recent years many new wineries have begun operations in most of the state's viticultural regions. There are approximately 800 wineries in California at this time, and the state produces 377 million gallons of wine—91 percent of all the wine produced in the United States. Statistics show that Californians drink 94.9 million gallons of wine annually, or 3.07 gallons per person.

Some concerns within the California wine industry are: a new type of phylloxera that has been discovered attacking the state's vineyards; economic troubles that closed many wineries in the early 1990s; problems created by tourism and land development that have given rise to zoning and building restrictions limiting winery and vineyard expansion; and continuing debates over how to balance the health benefits and risks involved in drinking alcoholic beverages. The latter has been researched and debated; the most recent conclusion by the medical field is that a moderate amount of red wine daily actually helps to prevent heart attacks.

California Wines

There are two main categories of California wines: varietal and generic. In accordance with current laws, varietal wines contain at least 75 percent of one grape variety (such as Cabernet Sauvignon), and they are labeled with the name of that grape. Generic wines, on the other hand, can be made from almost any blend of grapes. If the terms generic and varietal are unfamiliar, associating them with "general" and "variety" may help keep them straight. Although inexpensive generic wines may bear labels like "Chablis" or "Burgundy" (which are, strictly speaking, areas of France, as are Champagne and Bordeaux), a small group of winemakers has developed a keen interest in the classic Bordeaux-type blends. This kind of wine is sometimes referred to as Meritage or "claret," and fine examples can be found at Cosentino, Cain, and Robert Sinskey, among others.

Vintage date and origin also help identify wines. A date on the label indicates that at least 95 percent of the wine is from grapes harvested that season. This enables you to recognize wines produced in good years, when the climate has been particularly favorable, and to avoid the occasional vintage that may have suffered from excessive heat or early rain. (But don't forget that great wines can be made in "poor" years.) Another signpost of quality is the name of a premium growing region, like Napa Valley, on the label. When these American viticulture areas (AVA) appear on the label, it indicates the origin of at least 85 percent of the grapes in that wine.

If you intend to serve wine with a meal, you will probably want a *table wine*. This most familiar type has an alcohol content of between 7 and 15 percent. It may be red, white or pink (rosé). Red wines, which tend to be dry and full-bodied, are generally served with red meats and other hearty foods. White table wines are more delicate and range from dry to sweet; they are often enjoyed by themselves as well as with meals (particularly fish, fowl and light meat dishes), and the sweetest varieties go well with dessert. Rosé wines, served with almost any dish, are especially suited to casual dining. Modified according to your own preferences, these guidelines will help you select a wine that complements your meal.

Sparkling wines are table wines that have undergone a second fermentation to make them effervescent. The most popular is styled after French Champagne and is labeled according to its sweetness: Natural is extremely dry, with Brut, Extra Dry, and Sec progressively sweeter.

Aperitif and dessert wines have a higher alcohol content, between 17 and 21 percent. Served before meals, aperitif wines include dry sherry and vermouth. Sweet sherries, port and numerous late-harvest varietals are considered dessert wines, to be served after meals.

Unlike the other categories, *fruit and berry wines* are not produced from grapes but from other types of fruit, such as strawberries, apricots or cherries. They tend to be sweet, with an alcohol content that is generally 12 percent but may be as high as 20 percent.

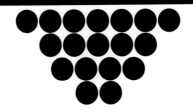

Winery Listings

Southern California

Southern California was once the center of California winemaking. In 1769 missionaries planted their first vineyard at Mission San Diego; 70 years later, grape growing was the major industry in the Los Angeles area. The Cucamonga Valley's warm climate and sandy soil were also well-suited to inexpensive grape varieties such as Zinfandel and Mission. Eventually the vineyards in these areas gave way to suburban sprawl, but several of the original wineries in Southern California have remained in operation, such as Bernardo Winery (1889) in San Diego, Galleano Winery (1927) in Mira Loma, San Antonio Winery (1917) in Los Angeles, J. Filippi Winery (1922) in the Rancho Cucamonga Valley, and Ferrara Winery (1932) in Escondido.

In the Escondido area, only a few hundred acres of vineyards remain; however, just 30 miles north lie the rolling hills of Temecula, covered with young vineyards. This terrain lies below the highest mountains of all five Southern California counties and is a unique microclimate that, at a 1500-foot elevation, inspires cool afternoon and evening summer breezes. This, and the well-drained soils of the area, combine to produce premium grapes such as Cabernet Sauvignon and white Riesling. The area's 13 wineries comprise the now-recognized Temecula Valley Wine Country.

OF SPECIAL INTEREST

OLD TOWN TEMECULA MAINSTREET ASSOCIATION
28636 Front St., Ste. 106, Temecula 92390. (909) 699-8138; FAX (909) 699-1148. Open daily 9 a.m. to 5 p.m.

In addition to tourist information, maps are offered for a downtown walking tour, the antique shopping district and wine country.

ROBERT MONDAVI WINE & FOOD CENTER
1570 Scenic Ave., Costa Mesa 92626. (714) 979-4510; FAX (714) 979-5616. Tours are available by appointment.

Mondavi's philosophy is to promote education about wine and food. They offer cooking classes, wine seminars and tastings, art shows with wine and food, and special-event dinners. The center is surrounded by a rose garden terrace and a one-acre sculpture garden.

SUNRISE BALLOONS
Mailing address: P.O. Box 891360, Temecula 92589. (800) 548-9912. Open daily including holidays. Fares range from $85 to $160 per person. Reservations required.

Hot air balloon rides over the Temecula area include beverages and snacks. Rides last approximately one hour, weather permitting, and are accessible to the handicapped. Also offered are horse-drawn carriage tours through the back roads of the wineries; prices start at $150 per person.

TEMECULA SHUTTLE WINE COUNTRY TOURS
41873 Moreno Rd., Temecula 92390. (909) 695-9999. Open daily 12:30 to 4:30 p.m. Closed major holidays. Per-person fares begin at $42.50. Reservations required.

Personalized, narrated, four-hour van tours visit four Temecula Valley wineries. Departures require a minimum of six passengers. Fare includes light lunch, champagne and wine tastings.

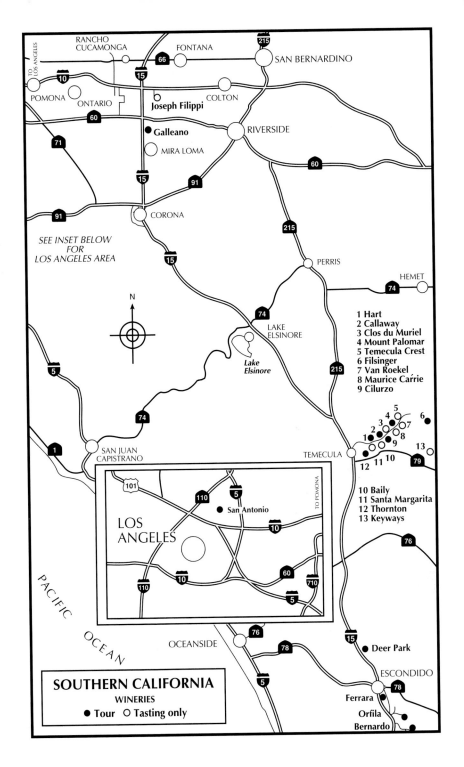

RANCHO CUCAMONGA
FONTANA
215
SAN BERNARDINO
66
15
TO LOS ANGELES
10
POMONA
ONTARIO
COLTON
Joseph Filippi
60
71
Galleano
RIVERSIDE
15
MIRA LOMA
60
91
91
CORONA
215
SEE INSET BELOW
FOR
LOS ANGELES AREA
15
PERRIS
HEMET
74
74
N
LAKE
ELSINORE

1 Hart
2 Callaway
3 Clos du Muriel
4 Mount Palomar
5 Temecula Crest
6 Filsinger
7 Van Roekel
8 Maurice Carrie
9 Cilurzo

5
215
Lake
Elsinore
74
5
3 4
2
7
6
1
8
74
9
1
SAN JUAN
CAPISTRANO
13
TEMECULA
10
12 11
79

101
110
5
TO POMONA
San Antonio
LOS
ANGELES
10
60
710
110
10
5

10 Baily
11 Santa Margarita
12 Thornton
13 Keyways

76

PACIFIC
76
OCEAN
OCEANSIDE
78
15
Deer Park
ESCONDIDO
5
78

SOUTHERN CALIFORNIA
WINERIES
● Tour   ○ Tasting only

Ferrara
Orfila
Bernardo

WINERIES IN SOUTHERN CALIFORNIA

BAILY VINEYARD & WINERY

36150 Pauba Rd., Temecula 92592. Tasting room 5 miles east off I-15 at 33833 Rancho California Rd., Temecula 92591. (909) 676-9463. Open for tasting daily 10 a.m. to 5 p.m. Closed Jan. 1, Thanksgiving and Dec. 25. $2.25 tasting fee for five wines includes logo glass.

Carol and Phil Baily moved to Temecula in 1981 and found grapes growing all around their property. Deciding to try their hand at winemaking, they spent a few years attempting to make it at home. A friend told them that it was a lot easier to make good wine commercially, and in 1986 they opened a winery and vineyard. Taking courses at UC Davis in winemaking greatly improved their skills; they mainly use a "hands off" technique of letting the wine progress with as little intervention as possible. Their wines have won awards at major competitions. The winery produces 4000 cases annually of Cabernet Sauvignon, Sauvignon Blanc, Sémillon Riesling Blend, Muscat Blanc, Red Generic, late-harvest White Riesling and Cabernet Blanc. There are picnic facilities, gift items for purchase and a view of the entire valley. The Bailys and several local friends purchased Britton Cellars and have started a new winery, Temecula Crest Winery (see listing).

BERNARDO WINERY

7 miles southeast of Escondido off Pomerado Rd. at 13330 Paseo del Verano Norte, San Diego 92128. (619) 487-1866. Open for tasting and self-guided tours daily 9 a.m. to 5 p.m. Patio restaurant open Tue. through Sun., 11 a.m. to 3 p.m.

Bernardo, founded in 1889, is located in a complex of art, gift and specialty shops. The oldest winery in San Diego County, the original wood aging vats

Callaway Vineyard & Winery's modern tasting room and gift shop is situated on a hilltop with an expansive view of the valley and vineyards.

are still in use and the winery has maintained several of its vineyards. All Bernardo wines—dessert and table—are sold exclusively through the retail store on the premises.

CALLAWAY VINEYARD & WINERY

4 miles east of Temecula at 32720 Rancho California Rd., 92589. (909) 676-4001; FAX (909) 676-5209. Open for tasting daily 10:30 a.m. to 5 p.m. Tours Mon. through Fri. at 11 a.m., 1 and 3 p.m.; Sat. and Sun. from 11 a.m. to 4 p.m. Closed Jan. 1, Easter, Thanksgiving and Dec. 25. $3 tasting fee includes souvenir glass.

A long, paved driveway flanked by varieties of rose bushes leads up the hill to the 720-acre winery and vineyard,

originally planted in 1969. Its location has the advantage of cool coastal breezes and a microclimate suitable for premium grape production. Built in 1973, the winery was designed to incorporate modern equipment and techniques. A gift shop, refrigerated deli items and picnic facilities are available to visitors.

CILURZO VINEYARD & WINERY

5½ miles east of Temecula off Rancho California Rd. at 41220 Calle Contento, Temecula 92592. (909) 676-5250. Open for tasting and self-guided tours daily 9:30 a.m. to 4:45 p.m. $1 tasting fee refunded with purchase.

Vincenzo and Audrey Cilurzo bought their Temecula property in 1967 as a haven from Vincenzo's high-pressure Hollywood career, and in 1978 they began making wine. Annual production ranges between 8000 and 10,000 cases per year. Four white and three red varietals, a chianti-style proprietary blend and a late-harvest Petite Sirah make up the current offerings of the Cilurzos and winemaker Larry Evilsizer. There are gift items for purchase and a tree-shaded picnic area that overlooks a small lake with ducks.

CLOS DU MURIEL VINEYARDS & WINERY

33410 Rancho California Rd., Temecula 92590. (909) 676-5400; FAX (909) 676-9606. Open for tasting daily 10 a.m. to 5 p.m. Tours are self-guided. Closed Jan. 1, Thanksgiving and Dec. 25. $4 tasting fee for all wines includes a souvenir glass.

Grape stomping just for fun at Callaway Vineyard and Winery.

Nadja Djekich

Established in 1989, the winery focuses on Temecula, Napa and Sonoma wines. Annual production is 25,000 cases of red, white, sweet, Rhône and Bordeaux wines. Entertainment on Saturday and Sunday. Picnic facilities and refrigerated deli items are available for visitors.

DEER PARK ESCONDIDO
1 mile south of Gopher Canyon Rd. at 29013 Champagne Blvd., Escondido 92026. (619) 749-1666. Open for tasting daily 10 a.m. to 5 p.m. Automobile museum is open daily 10 a.m. to 4 p.m. Museum admission $5 per adult, $3 per senior, age 12 and under free.

This microwinery produces 450 cases of Chardonnay per year from its 3½-acre vineyard, and the crushing and pressing equipment is similarly small scale. Winery owner Robert Knapp has a collection of convertible automobiles dating from 1903 to 1976, which he displays in the museum. Several picnic areas are located throughout the grounds, and refrigerated deli items are sold in the spacious tasting room.

FERRARA WINERY
1120 W. 15th Ave., Escondido 92025. (619) 745-7632. Open for tasting and self-guided tours daily 10 a.m. to 5 p.m. Closed Jan. 1, Easter, Thanksgiving and Dec. 25.

The Ferrara Winery is located on a five-acre plot on the west side of Escondido. Founded in 1932 and appointed a State Historical Point of Interest in 1971, the facility blends traditional and contemporary motifs: old redwood tanks contrast with a modern stainless steel stemmer-crusher. The Ferrara family produces both varietal and generic wines, which can be sampled in the tasting room.

FILSINGER WINERY & VINEYARDS
11 miles east of Temecula off SR 79 at 39050 De Portola Rd., Temecula 92592. (909) 676-4594. Open for tasting Sat. and Sun. from 10:30 a.m. to 5 p.m. Tours by appointment. $1 tasting fee.

William Filsinger's ancestors were German winemakers, and in 1972 he renewed his ties to that part of his heritage by purchasing property in Temecula and planting vines. The winery was built eight years later, and today it produces Cabernet Sauvignon, Chardonnay, Gamay Beaujolais, Gewürztraminer, Johannisberg Riesling, Sauvignon Blanc and White Zinfandel. In 1990 Filsinger released its first sparkling wines, which are made using the *méthode champenoise*. Winery production is about 8000 cases per year. Gift items are available for purchase, and visitors may picnic at the shaded tables.

GALLEANO WINERY
4231 Wineville Rd., Mira Loma 91752. (909) 685-5376. Open for tasting Mon. through Sat. 9 a.m. to 5 p.m., Sun. 10:30 a.m. to 5 p.m. Tours Sat. and Sun. between 2 and 4 p.m. and by appointment.

Domenico Galleano immigrated from Northern Italy in 1913. In 1927 he purchased the Cantu Ranch from Ana Cantu, whose husband, Colonel Esteban Cantu, served as governor of Baja California from 1917 to 1920. The winery has been a Galleano family enterprise ever since. The two-story house, a barn and outbuildings were built between 1895 and 1910; they remain largely in their original condition and collectively have been designated a County Historical Landmark. Galleano features wines of almost every variety: aperitif, table, dessert and sparkling. A gift shop, refrigerated deli items, and a picnic area with farm animals are available to visitors.

HART WINERY

4 miles east of Temecula at 41300 Avenida Biona (mailing address: P.O. Box 956, 92593). (909) 676-6300. Open for tasting daily 9 a.m. to 4:30 p.m. Tours upon request. $2 tasting fee includes logo glass.

This small family winery was built in 1980 adjacent to an 11-acre vineyard. Hart specializes in handcrafted, barrel-aged red wines and full-bodied white wines. Cabernet Sauvignon, Merlot, Mourvedre, Syrah and Sauvignon Blanc are produced from estate-grown and purchased grapes.

JOSEPH FILIPPI WINERY

12647 Base Line Rd., Rancho Cucamonga 91739. (909) 899-5755; FAX (909) 428-6264. Open daily 10 a.m. to 7 p.m. Two other locations open daily 10 a.m. to 6 p.m.: tasting only at Guasti-Ontario, 2803 E. Guasti Rd., (909) 390-6998; tasting and tours by appointment at 11211 S. Etiwanda Ave., Fontana, (909) 428-8638. Closed Jan. 1, Thanksgiving and Dec. 25.

The Filippis immigrated from Northern Italy to Rancho Cucamonga in 1922. They chose the site of early 1900s Regina Winery (which had produced champagne, cooking wines and wine vinegars) to plant their first vines. Today it is a historical landmark and the three Filippi brothers (J.P., Gino and James) are the fourth generation to operate the winery. The tasting room has a unique bar made of a 20,000-gallon, redwood wine-aging tank. The 40,000-case annual production includes Ports, Gewürztraminer, French Colombard, Sauvignon Blanc, Sherries, Cucamonga Cooler Wine Spritzers, Red and White Zinfandels, and a dessert wine, Angelica. Rancho Cucamonga and the Guasti facility (the site of the 1904 Brookside Winery) both feature historical displays, tree-shaded picnic areas and deli items.

KEYWAYS WINERY & VINEYARD

37338 De Portola Rd., Temecula 92592. (909) 676-1451, (909) 676-2152. Open for tasting daily 10 a.m. to 5 p.m. $1 fee.

Built in 1987, Keyways produces 4000 cases of Zinfandel annually. A large display of antiques, a picnic area and catering are available by reservation.

MAURICE CARRIE WINERY

34225 Rancho California Rd., Temecula 92591. (909) 676-1711; FAX (909) 676-8397. Open for tasting daily 10 a.m. to 5 p.m.

Bud and Maurice Carrie decided to retire and grow grapes for other wineries in 1984. In 1986 they decided to produce their own wine, and now annual production is 40,000 cases of 17 different varietal wines. The old barn and windmill on the property are depicted on their label. A gift shop, refrigerated deli items, a picnic area and children's playground are available to visitors. They also have another winery ¹⁄₁₀ mile up the road, Van Roeckel Vineyards (see listing).

MOUNT PALOMAR WINERY

5 miles east of Temecula at 33820 Rancho California Rd., 92591. (909) 676-5047; FAX (909) 694-5688. Open for tasting daily 9 a.m. to 6 p.m., Oct. through Mar. to 5 p.m. Tours Mon. through Fri. at 1:30 and 3:30 p.m.; Sat. and Sun. at 11:30 a.m., 1:30 and 3:30 p.m. Closed Jan. 1, Easter, Thanksgiving and Dec. 25. $2 tasting fee includes logo glass.

Mount Palomar was one of the first wineries founded in the Temecula area, with vineyards established in 1969 and the winery in 1975. Today, the winery produces 14,000 cases per year of handcrafted wines ranging from classic to unique varietals: Chardonnay, Merlot, Johannisberg Riesling, Syrah, Sangiovese, White Zinfandel and Cream Sherry. The full service, Mediterranean-style deli is open Friday through Sunday, and picnic items can be purchased daily. Visitors are invited to visit the gift shop and use several picnic areas and the covered pavilion.

ORFILA VINEYARDS & WINERY
6 miles southeast of Escondido on I-15 and Via Rancho Pkwy. at 13455 San Pasqual Rd., San Diego 92025. (619) 738-6500. Open for tasting and tours daily; Jun. through Aug. 10 a.m. to 6 p.m., rest of year to 5 p.m. Tours at 11:30 a.m., 1:30, 3 and 4 p.m.

Previously the Thomas Jaeger Winery, it is now owned by A. Orfila, who served for 15 years as Argentina's Ambassador to the United States. Italian-born winemaker Leon N. Santoro is the director of the winery, which now produces about 13,000 cases each year of Merlot, Chardonnay, Sauvignon Blanc, Sangiovese and Syrah; a Viognier is also planned. There are a shaded picnic arbor and indoor tables for visitor use during inclement weather; picnic items are sold in the gift shop.

SAN ANTONIO WINERY, INC.
737 Lamar St., Los Angeles 90031. (213) 223-1401. A second location is off the 60 freeway at 2801 S. Milliken, Ontario 91765. (909) 947-3995. Open for tasting and tours daily 10:30 a.m. to 6 p.m. Tours on the hour 10 a.m. to 2 p.m. Closed major holidays.

Santo Cambianica founded his winery in 1917 in what is now the industrial district of Los Angeles. Today it is a thriving family business offering varietal wines made from grapes of the Napa and Sonoma counties and the

Monterey coast. A restaurant on the premises serves northern Italian and continental dishes which can be enjoyed inside or in the winery's tree-shaded park. The wine and gift shop carry a variety of wines (including other labels) and related gifts. The Ontario location has 10 acres of vineyards, a tasting room, gift shop, deli section, and an indoor and outdoor picnic area. A small animal farm has llamas, sheep, pheasants, chickens, turkeys and deer. It adjoins a country farm area that grows produce.

SANTA MARGARITA WINERY
33490 Madera de Playa, Temecula 92592. (909) 676-4431. Open for tasting, Mon. through Fri. by appointment, Sat. and Sun. from 11 a.m. to 4:30 p.m.

Santa Margarita specializes in aged Cabernet Sauvignon wines.

TEMECULA CREST WINERY
40620 Calle Contento, Temecula 92591. (909) 676-8231; FAX (909) 676-8356. Open for tasting and tours daily 10 a.m. to 5 p.m. Tours for groups of 20 or more by appointment only. Closed Jan. 1, Thanksgiving and Dec. 25. $2.25 tasting fee for five wines includes a logo glass.

Previously called Clos du Muriel, Temecula Crest Winery was renamed by Carol and Phil Baily, owners of Bailys Vineyard & Winery, and a group of local professionals who are also avid wine enthusiasts. Production is 4000 cases annually, focusing on premium wines with outstanding varietal character from grapes that are estate-grown. Wines produced are Chardonnay, Cabernet Sauvignon, Sauvignon Blanc, White Riesling, Cabernet Blanc, Merlot, Nebbiolo, late-harvest Sauvignon Blanc, and a proprietary blend of Sauvignon Blanc and White Riesling called "Contento."

There is a spectacular view of the San Jacinto Valley from the winery. Carol Baily prepares special six-course winemaker dinners in the Barrel Room, with each course matched to a different Temecula Crest Wine. Twice a year "Jazz on the Green" features a jazz recording artist and a barbecue dinner. There are wine-related gift items available for purchase.

THORNTON WINERY
32575 Rancho California Rd., Temecula (mailing address: P.O. Box 9008, 92589-9008). (909) 699-0099; FAX (909) 699-5536; special event line (909) 699-3021. Open for tasting daily 10 a.m. to 5 p.m. Tours Sat. and Sun. only. Champagne bar open Mon. through Fri. noon to 4 p.m., Sat. and Sun. 11 a.m. to 5 p.m. Cafe Champagne open daily 11 a.m. to 9 p.m. $6 tasting fee.

This impressive stone and slate facility in the Temecula Valley is situated on a hill with its own waterfall. It is the only Southern California winery specializing in *méthode champenoise* sparkling wine, producing Culbertson sparkling wine and Brindiamo premium varietal wines. A view of the bottling facility can be seen through a special glass window in the gift shop. The restaurant has an outdoor seating area in the cobblestone courtyard, which has a handsome stone fountain as its centerpiece. A shaded picnic area is available to visitors.

VAN ROEKEL VINEYARDS
34567 Rancho California Rd., Temecula 92591. (909) 699-6961. Open for tasting daily 10 a.m. to 5 p.m.

Owned by Bud and Maurice Cafrie of Maurice Cafrie Winery (see listing), Van Roekel is Temecula's newest winery, specializing in premium wines. Deli items, gourmet cheeses and a large selection of wine-related gifts are available. There is a picnic area for visitors.

WITCH CREEK WINERY
North of Main St. at the KO Corral, 2608 B St., Julian 92036. (619) 789-3024. Tasting room tentatively open daily 11 a.m. to 5 p.m. (call to confirm). $2 tasting fee.

The Witch Creek tasting room opened in 1994 and specializes in red wines such as Cabernet Sauvignon; also produced are blushes and whites. Gift items and packaged foods are available.

ANNUAL EVENTS

Exact dates, prices and other information about the events listed below may be verified by calling the telephone numbers shown. In addition, some wineries individually sponsor special brunches, dinners and summer concerts; for information on events sponsored by a particular winery, call that winery and ask if a calendar of events is available.

FEBRUARY—

BARREL TASTING
Various wineries, Temecula (mailing address: Temecula Valley Vintners' Association, P.O. Box 1601, 92390). (909) 699-3626.

Wine from the barrel is paired with gourmet foods and hors d'oeuvres at participating wineries. Tickets to this two-day, valley-wide event include a commemorative glass.

LOYOLA MARYMOUNT UNIVERSITY WINE CLASSIC
Loyola Marymount University, Los Angeles. (310) 338-3065. Admission $50.

Wine tasting is provided by more than 45 premium California wineries. Admission includes a souvenir wine glass, wine tasting and a buffet of cheeses, patés, fruits and breads.

APRIL—

TEMECULA BALLOON AND WINE FESTIVAL

Lake Skinner, Temecula (mailing address: Temecula Valley Balloon & Wine Association, 27475 Ynez Rd., Ste. 335, 92591). (909) 676-6713. Admission $10. Reservations required for balloon rides.

Hot air balloons are launched and wine tasting takes place throughout one weekend. Food and beverage booths, live entertainment, arts and crafts exhibits and a Kids Faire round out the family activities.

MAY—

WINE & JAZZ

Temecula Crest Winery, Temecula. (909) 676-8231. Admission $20.

A Saturday evening of jazz accompanies a barbecue dinner with wine.

AUGUST—

WINE & JAZZ

Temecula Crest Winery, Temecula. (909) 676-8231. Admission $20.

A Saturday evening of jazz accompanies a barbecue dinner with wine.

NOVEMBER—

NOUVEAU CELEBRATION

Various wineries, Temecula (mailing address: Temecula Valley Vintners' Association, P.O. Box 1601, 92390). (909) 699-3626. Admission $30.

This two-day, valley-wide event during the third weekend of the month celebrates the release of the new wines of the harvest paired with gourmet foods.

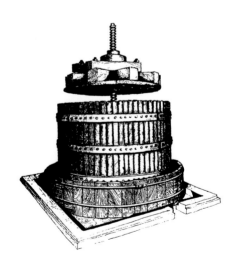

Central Coast

The Central Coast is a designated viticultural area that includes San Luis Obispo, Santa Barbara and Ventura counties. Due to the unusual east-west transverse range of the Santa Ynez Mountains along the Pacific Coast, a flow of cooling ocean breezes and fog rolls through the gaps in the mountains into four valleys: Santa Maria, Edna, Santa Ynez and Los Alamos. This creates superior microclimates that are ideal for growing every type of grape. The University of California at Davis verified these ideal conditions for the growth of premium grape varieties in Santa Barbara County, especially Chardonnay, Riesling and Pinot Noir.

The warmer Santa Ynez Valley, a subappellation of the Central Coast, lies within Santa Barbara County; the Santa Maria Valley is divided between Santa Barbara and San Luis Obispo counties. These counties were important wine producing areas a century ago and today there are more than 30 wineries in Santa Barbara County.

A boom in viticulture occurred in San Luis Obispo County for similar reasons—the favorable climate with sea breezes and fogs moderating summer temperatures, good soil and land availability. A number of new vineyards and wineries are demonstrating the region's suitability for premium wine production. The county is home to some of the oldest California wineries, which have traditionally emphasized Zinfandel and generic table wines. Designated viticultural areas within the county include the Edna Valley, Paso Robles and York Mountain.

OF SPECIAL INTEREST

LOS OLIVOS WINE & SPIRITS EMPORIUM
2531 Grand Ave., Los Olivos (mailing address: P.O. Box 783, 93441). (805) 688-4409, (805) 687-1024. Open for tasting daily 11 a.m. to 6 p.m.

This establishment is located in the historic Los Olivos Market and is the tasting room for more than 10 wineries: Alban Vineyards, Kalyra, Lane Tanner, Chimère, Makor, Fiddlehead Cellars, Qupé, Whitcraft Winery, Germain-Robin and St. George Spirits.

WINERIES IN THE CENTRAL COAST

ADELAIDA CELLARS
5½ miles off Nacimiento Lake Dr. at 5805 Adelaida Rd., Paso Robles 93446. (805) 239-8980. Open for tasting daily 11 a.m. *to 5 p.m. Tours for 15 or more by appointment. $2 tasting fee.*

Housed in leased facilities, John Munch crushed his first vintage in 1981. It took him four moves and another 10 years to finally build his own winery. He produces Cabernet Sauvignon, Chardonnay, Pinot Noir, Syrah and Zinfandel, all from low-yield mountain vineyards west of Paso Robles in San Luis Obispo County. Munch prefers to work with fruit from dry-farmed vineyards and believes winemaking has more in common with cooking than chemistry—his rich, intensely flavorful wines attest to this philosophy. An amphitheater on Fair Oaks Mountain above the winery provides a setting for musical entertainment and special dinners. Munch's wife Andree makes Le Cuvier wines.

ARCIERO WINERY
6 miles east of Paso Robles on SR 46 (mailing address: P.O. Box 1287,

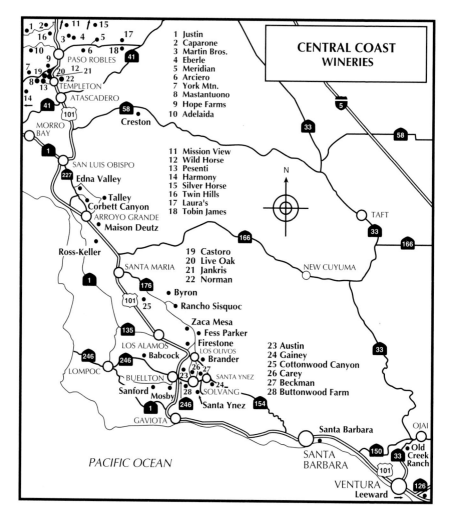

CENTRAL COAST
WINERIES

1 Justin
2 Caparone
3 Martin Bros.
4 Eberle
5 Meridian
6 Arciero
7 York Mtn.
8 Mastantuono
9 Hope Farms
10 Adelaida

11 Mission View
12 Wild Horse
13 Pesenti
14 Harmony
15 Silver Horse
16 Twin Hills
17 Laura's
18 Tobin James

19 Castoro
20 Live Oak
21 Jankris
22 Norman

23 Austin
24 Gainey
25 Cottonwood Canyon
26 Carey
27 Beckman
28 Buttonwood Farm

93447). (805) 239-2562. *Open for tasting and self-guided tours daily 10 a.m. to 5 p.m., Jun. through Aug. on Sat. and Sun. to 6 p.m.*

This modern estate winery of Mediterranean design was built in 1986 in the rolling foothills east of Paso Robles. The facility overlooks more than 500 acres of estate vineyards, where grapes for nine varietal wines are produced. Five acres of landscaping includes a rose garden, fountain and picnic area. On display are the Arciero family's retired race cars. Refrigerated picnic items are for sale in the gift shop. The winery hosts summer concerts.

AUSTIN CELLARS

2923 Grand Ave., Los Olivos (mailing address: P.O. Box 636, 93441). (805) 688-9665. Open for tasting daily 11 a.m. to 6 p.m. Closed Dec 25.

Open since 1981, Austin Cellars is located in town in a converted old residence. They produce Sauvignon Blanc, Pinot Noir, Chardonnay and dessert wines.

BABCOCK VINEYARDS

9½ miles west of US 101 at 5175 SR 246, Lompoc 93436. (805) 736-1455. Open for tasting and tours Fri., Sat. and Sun. 10:30 a.m. to 4 p.m. or by appointment.

This small family winery sits at the western edge of the Santa Ynez Valley in the Santa Rosa Hills. Winemaker Bryan Babcock produces about 10,000 cases a year of Chardonnay, Gewürztraminer, Pinot Noir, Riesling, Sauvignon Blanc and Sangiovese from 50 acres of estate vineyards in Santa Barbara County. There is a shaded picnic area for visitors.

BECKMAN VINEYARDS

Off US 101 via SR 154 at 2670 Ontiveros Rd., Los Olivos (mailing address: P.O. Box 542, 93441). (805) 688-8664. Open for tasting daily 10 a.m. to 4 p.m.

In view of the beautiful Santa Ynez Mountains, this 17-acre vineyard produces Sauvignon Blanc, Chardonnay, Cabernet Sauvignon and Rosé. There is a picnic area with a covered gazebo by a duck pond.

BRANDER VINEYARD

2 miles southeast of Los Olivos off SR 154 (mailing address: P.O. Box 92, 93441). (805) 688-2455; FAX (805) 688-8010. Open for tasting daily 10 a.m. to 5 p.m. Group tours by appointment. $2.50 tasting fee.

The 40-acre Brander Vineyard was planted in 1975, and the winery was built five years later. Annual production is 8000 cases of estate-bottled varietals under the Brander label; the emphasis is on the house specialties, Sauvignon Blanc and Bordeaux-type blends. A second label is used for non-estate-bottled wine.

BUTTONWOOD FARM WINERY

1½ miles northeast of Solvang at 1500 Alamo Pintado Rd., 93469. (805) 688-3032; FAX (805) 688-3032. Open for tasting daily 11 a.m. to 5 p.m. $2.50 fee includes logo glass.

This 106-acre, family operated winery produced their first vintage in 1989. The land is divided between an ancient river bed–used for organic fruit, vegetables, herbs and flowers–and a higher mesa area where the vineyards are situated. The winery produces 5000 cases of Sauvignon Blanc, Merlot, Cabernet Sauvignon, Cabernet Franc, Marsanne and various blends. There is a gift shop for visitors.

BYRON VINEYARD & WINERY

12 miles southeast of Santa Maria at 5230 Tepusquet Rd., 93454. (805) 937-7288. Open for tasting and informal tours daily 10 a.m. to 4 p.m. Closed major holidays.

Byron Vineyard & Winery crushed its first vintage in 1984 under winemaker Byron "Ken" Brown. The winery focuses its efforts on Chardonnay and Pinot Noir and produces limited quantities of Pinot Blanc, Pinot Gris and Sauvignon Blanc. Most of the grapes are grown on Byron's 641-acre Santa Maria Valley estate, which includes the Nielson Vineyard, Santa Barbara County's oldest commercial vineyard, planted in 1964. The charming, intimate tasting room offers a wide array of fine gifts and gourmet foods. Visitors may use a landscaped picnic area and deck overlooking the estate vineyards and picturesque Tepusquet Canyon.

CAPARONE

North of Paso Robles via Nacimiento Lake Dr. (CR G14), then 1½ miles east to 2280 San Marcos Rd., 93446. (805) 467-3827. Open for tasting and tours daily 11 a.m. to 5 p.m.

Dave Caparone makes only unfiltered, unfined red wines of intense varietal character—Brunello, Cabernet Sauvignon, Merlot, Nebbiolo and Zinfandel. Processing is limited to racking—a laborious and time-consuming but traditional method of clarifying wine.

CAREY CELLARS
2 miles east of Solvang off SR 246 at 1711 Alamo Pintado Rd., 93463. (805) 688-8554. Open for tasting and tours daily 10 a.m. to 4 p.m.

Carey Cellars is what most people think a winery should be: rustic and off the beaten path, with a focus on making first-class wines. The winery is housed in an antique red barn surrounded by estate vineyards. The tasting room is in a small farm house built in 1926. Wines include Cabernet, Merlot, Chardonnay, Sauvignon Blanc and Muscat. A shaded picnic area is available to visitors.

CASTORO CELLARS
1¼ miles west of US 101 at 1315 N. Bethel Rd., Templeton 93465. (805) 238-2602. Open for tasting daily 11 a.m. to 5:30 p.m. $2 tasting fee reimbursed with wine purchase.

This beautiful 15-acre vineyard produces 15,000 cases annually of Merlot, Chardonnay and Cabernet, with special focus on reds and Zinfandel. Visitors may use the picnic facilities and visit the gift shop.

CORBETT CANYON VINEYARDS
8 miles southeast of San Luis Obispo off SR 227 at 2195 Corbett Canyon Rd. (mailing address: P.O. Box 3159, 93403). (805) 544-5800. Open for tasting Sun. through Thur. 10 a.m. to 4:30 p.m.; Fri. and Sat. 10 a.m. to 5 p.m. Tours Sat. and Sun. only by appointment.

The first winery in southern San Luis Obispo County was established in 1979 and it is the largest in the county.

Corbett Canyon produces 300,000 cases per year of Cabernet Sauvignon, Sauvignon Blanc, White Zinfandel, Chardonnay and Pinot Noir. A gift shop, art gallery, deli items and a picnic area are available.

COTTONWOOD CANYON VINEYARD & WINERY
3940 Dominion Rd., Santa Maria 93454 (mailing address: P.O. Box 3459, San Luis Obispo 93403). (805) 937-9063. Open for tasting 10 a.m. to 5 p.m. Guided tours. $2 tasting fee includes logo glass.

Set amid oak, eucalyptus and cotton-wood trees, the vineyard receives ocean effects of wind and fog on a daily basis. These affects extend the growing season by six weeks, and in addition to the technique of removing leaves for more exposure and hand picking the berries, adds a "fruity bouquet and taste" to its wines. The Beko family produces 4000 cases of Chardonnay and Pinot Noir annually. There are picnic facilities and a gift shop.

CRESTON VINEYARDS
Winery on SR 58 at milepost 17 (mailing address: Star Rt., Hwy. 58, Creston 93432). Tasting room in Templeton, 5 miles south of Paso Robles at US 101 and Vineyard Dr. (805) 238-7398; FAX (805) 434-1399. Tasting room in Templeton open daily 10 a.m. to 5 p.m. Tours and tasting at the winery location are by appointment only.

Larry and Stephanie Rosenbloom bought the Indian Creek Ranch in 1980, and in 1982 they began building a winery on the 479-acre property. Set high in the La Panza mountains, the area still looks and feels like ranchland. Creston Vineyards produces about 14,000 cases per year of Cabernet Sauvignon, Chardonnay, Sauvignon Blanc, Chevrier Blanc, White Zinfandel, Merlot, Zinfandel and Pinot Noir. The road to the winery is winding

and narrow in spots and is not
recommended for trailers.

EBERLE WINERY
*3½ miles east of Paso Robles on SR 46
(mailing address: P.O. Box 2459,
93447). (805) 238-9607; FAX (805)
237-0344. Open for tasting daily May
through Sept. 10 a.m. to 6 p.m., Oct.
through Apr. to 5 p.m. Tours by
appointment.*

Gary Eberle's modern, wood-sided
winery sits atop a small rise just east of
Paso Robles. The 12,000-case annual
production of Chardonnay, Cabernet
Sauvignon, Muscat Canelli, Barbera,
Syrah and Zinfandel is made primarily
from estate-grown grapes. The large
tasting room is designed so that visitors
can oversee the winery operations
through bay windows.

EDNA VALLEY VINEYARD
*5 miles southeast of San Luis Obispo off SR
227 at 2585 Biddle Ranch Rd., 93401.
(805) 544-9594. Open for tasting and
tours daily 10 a.m. to 4 p.m.*

The drought of 1976-1977 forced the
owners, Chalone Inc., to supplement
their harvest with grapes from Paragon
Vineyards of San Luis Obispo. In 1980
the two businesses joined together to
build the winery at Edna Valley
Vineyard. The focus is on Chardonnay;
Pinot Noir is also produced, along with
sparkling wine. All 700 acres of
vineyards are adjacent to this 55,000-
case-per-year winery. Picnic tables are
available in the herb garden, and
tours cover the entire winemaking
process.

FESS PARKER WINERY
*5 miles east of junction US 101 and Zaca
Station Rd. at 6200 Foxen Canyon Rd.,
Los Olivos (mailing address: P.O. Box
908, 93441). (805) 688-1545. Open for
tasting and tours daily; May through Sept.,
9 a.m. to 5 p.m. (tours 10 a.m. to 3:45*

*p.m.); Oct. through Apr., 9 a.m. to
4:30 p.m. (tours 10 a.m. to 3 p.m.).
Closed Jan. 1, Easter, Thanksgiving, and
Dec. 25.*

Renowned for his portrayal of both
Davey Crockett and Daniel Boone in
film and television, Fess Parker owns
this winery located in the pastoral Santa
Ynez Valley. A family operation, the
winery is on a 714-acre ranch. The
visitor center has Fess Parker memor-
abilia, gourmet and gift items and wines.
Fess Parker is sometimes there on
Sundays to autograph bottles. There is a
picnic area for visitors.

FIRESTONE VINEYARD
*8 miles north of Buellton via US 101 on
Zaca Station Rd. (mailing address: P.O.
Box 244, Los Olivos 93441). (805) 688-
3940. Open for tasting and tours daily 10
a.m. to 4 p.m.*

In 1973, Brooks Firestone (of the tire-
manufacturing family) planted vines
near Los Olivos, a region offering
climatic conditions similar to those of
the Napa Valley. The first harvest was
in 1975; production now includes
Riesling, Gewürztraminer, Sauvignon
Blanc, Chardonnay, Merlot and
Cabernet Sauvignon. A gift shop and
picnic facilities are available for
visitors.

THE GAINEY VINEYARD
*1 mile east at 3950 E. SR 246, Santa
Ynez (mailing address: P.O. Box 910,
93460). (805) 688-0558; FAX (805)
688-5864. Open for tasting and tours
daily 10 a.m. to 5 p.m. $2.50 tasting fee
includes souvenir glass.*

This modern winery was designed and
built with the visitor in mind; informative tours thoroughly cover all phases
of winemaking. The winery also offers
a scenic picnic area, a deli with a gourmet food section and in the summer, a
concert series.

Michelle De Lude

Equestrian events take place during the Santa Ynez Carriage Classic, held in April at Firestone Vineyard.

HARMONY CELLARS

3255 Harmony Valley Rd., Harmony (mailing address: P.O. Box 2502, 93435). (800) 432-9239. Open for tasting and self-guided tours daily 10 a.m. to 5 p.m.; Jun. through Aug. to 5:30 p.m. $1 tasting fee.

Chuck and Kim Mulligan's winery is situated on a hill above the town of Harmony, on land that has been in Kim's family for four generations; her great-grandfather, Giacomo Barloggio, was one of the founders of the town's creamery cooperative and used to make wine in his basement. The winery today produces 3500 cases of Chardonnay, Pinot Noir, Cabernet Sauvignon, White Zinfandel, Zinfandel Beaujolais (Zinjolais), Johannisberg Riesling and Christmas Blush. There are picnic facilities and a gift shop for visitors.

HOPE FARMS WINERY

1 mile west of US 101 on SR 46 at 2175 Arbor Rd., Paso Robles (mailing address: P.O. Box 3260, 93447). (805) 238-6979. Open for tasting daily 11 a.m. to 5 p.m. Tours by appointment. Closed major holidays. $2 fee includes souvenir glass.

Brothers Chuck and Paul Hope and their wives Marlyn and Janet have been growing grapes in San Luis Obispo County since 1978. In 1989 they founded their winery, and the best 10 percent of their crop is used for the annual production of 3800 cases of Hope Farms Chardonnay, Cabernet Sauvignon, Muscat Canelli, Zinfandel and White Zinfandel. Visitors may picnic in the gazebo or garden, and deli items are sold in the tasting room. A banquet facility and a bed and breakfast inn are available for visitors.

JANKRIS WINERY
West of Templeton off 101 via SR 46 to Bethel Rd. (mailing address: Rt. 2, Box 40, Bethel Rd., 93465). (805) 434-0319. Open for tasting daily 11 a.m. to 5:30 p.m. $2 includes logo glass.

Owners Mark and Paula Gendron's turn-of-the-century Victorian house is situated on 46 acres of vineyard in the rolling green hills of Templeton. Their winery's name is derived from their daughters' names, January and Kristin. This family owned winery produces 3300 cases annually of award-winning Chardonnay, Pinot Blanc, Pinot Noir, Zinfandel, Merlot, Merzin, Syrah, Gamay and White Zinfandel. A glass gazebo and an enclosed patio are used for special events; refrigerated deli items, a restaurant, gift shop and picnic facilities are available for visitors.

JUSTIN VINEYARDS & WINERY
West of Paso Robles via Nacimiento Lake Dr. (CR G14) to 11680 Chimney Rock Rd., 93446. (805) 238-6932. Open for tasting daily 10 a.m. to 6 p.m. Tours by appointment.

In 1982 Justin and Debby Baldwin purchased 160 acres in the Adelaida Valley, far off the beaten track of most Paso Robles wineries, and they set about creating a winery that would reward visitors for their long drive. About 10,000 cases per year of Cabernet Sauvignon, Cabernet Franc, Chardonnay, Merlot, Port Orange Muscat and Meritage blends are

Justin Vineyards & Winery is situated in a pastoral area of Paso Robles.

31

produced from estate-grown grapes. The winery's country French-style tasting room is set amidst an English garden; monthly Guest Chef Dinners are held in the tasting room. Visitors are welcome to picnic in the gardens adjacent to the winery. There is also a bed and breakfast inn.

LAURA'S VINEYARD
6 miles east of Paso Robles at 5620 SR 46 E., 93446 (mailing address: P.O. Box 304, San Miguel 93451). (805) 238-6300. Open for tasting daily 10 a.m. to 6 p.m.

Clifford Giacobine named his winery in memory of his mother, Laura. Her home accommodates the tasting room and gift shop, and tables for picnicking are available on the front lawn. Annual wine production of 5000 cases includes Cabernet Sauvignon, Chardonnay, Johannisberg Riesling, White Zinfandel and Syrah.

LEEWARD WINERY
2784 Johnson Dr., Ventura 93003. (805) 656-5054. Open for tasting and tours daily 10 a.m. to 4 p.m.

This small winery opened in 1979 in an unlikely location at Oxnard's Channel Islands Harbor; it moved to its present site in 1982. The owners purchase select lots of Cabernet Sauvignon, Chardonnay, Pinot Noir and Merlot grapes from Northern and Central California vineyards; production is currently 15,000 cases annually.

LIVE OAK VINEYARDS
1 mile west of US 101 on SR 46 at 1480 N. Bethel Rd., Templeton 93446. (805) 227-4766. Open for tasting daily 10 a.m. to 6 p.m.

Bill and Janie Alberts came to Paso Robles in 1981 and planted 66 acres of premium wine grapes. Bill Alberts' previous experience was with his family's Porter Winery in Healdsburg and his aunt's Zinfandel vineyard in

Northern California's Alexander Valley. The Live Oak winery produces Chardonnay, Sauvignon Blanc, White Zinfandel, Zinfandel, Merlot and Cabernet Sauvignon. The building housing the tasting room and gift shop was a one-room schoolhouse from 1886 to 1927. Local artists' watercolors are on display and picnickers may relax under the oaks.

MAISON DEUTZ WINERY
1 mile south off US 101 at 453 Deutz Dr., Arroyo Grande 93420. (805) 481-1763. Open for tasting Wed. through Mon. 11 a.m. to 5 p.m. Tours by appointment only. Closed Tues. and major holidays. $4 to $5 tasting fee includes choice of wine and appetizers.

The venerable French Champagne house of Deutz founded their California outpost in 1981 on the rolling hills south of Arroyo Grande. Vineyards of Pinot Blanc, Pinot Noir and Chardonnay were planted, and a modern gravity-flow winery was constructed. Sparkling wines alone are vinified, using only the traditional *méthode champenoise*.

MARTIN BROTHERS WINERY
1 mile east of Paso Robles off SR 46 at 2610 Buena Vista Dr., (mailing address: P.O. Box 2599, 93447). (805) 238-2520. Open for tasting daily 11 a.m. to dusk. Tours by appointment only.

On land that was once a dairy farm, the Martin family built their winery in 1981. They specialize in Italian varietals such as Moscato Allegro, Pinot Grigio, Chardonnay in Botti, Sangiovese il Palio, Nebbiolo, Nebbiolo Vecchio, Zinfandel la Primitiva, Cabernet Estrucso, Gemelli, Vin Santo, Primitivo Appassito and Grappa di Nebbiolo. Seasonal concerts are held in the outdoor amphitheater and picnic facilities are available for visitors.

MASTANTUONO WINERY
4 miles west at Vineyard Dr. and SR 46; 2720 Oak View Rd., Templeton 93465. (805) 238-0676. Open for tasting daily 10 a.m. to 6 p.m.

A fourth-generation winemaker, Pasquale (Pat) Mastantuono sold his furniture business in 1976 to pursue his dream of producing premium wines. Pat is best known for his distinct red wines, achieved through unique processing which uses no fining or filtering. The "Zinman," as Pat has been nicknamed, also produces Fumé Blanc, White Zinfandel, Cabernet Sauvignon, a quality champagne and a special after-dinner sipping wine called Muscat Canelli, winner of a double gold award. Annual production is 11,000 cases. Refrigerated deli items, a gift shop and picnic facilities are available.

MERIDIAN VINEYARDS
7 miles east of Paso Robles at 7000 SR 46 E. (mailing address: P.O. Box 3289, 93447). (805) 237-6000; FAX (805) 239-5715. Open for tasting Wed. through Mon. 10 a.m. to 5 p.m. Closed Tues., Jan. 1, Easter, Thanksgiving and Dec. 25.

Meridian is owned by Wine World Estates and produces Chardonnay, Sauvignon Blanc, Pinot Noir, Syrah, Cabernet Sauvignon and Zinfandel. Winemaker Chuck Ortman is dedicated to producing premium wines. A gift shop, refrigerated deli items and picnic facilities are available for visitors.

MISSION VIEW VINEYARDS AND WINERY
Tasting room 3 miles north of Paso Robles at US 101 and Wellsona Rd. (mailing address: P.O. Box 129, San Miguel 93451). (805) 467-3104. Open for tasting daily 10 a.m. to 5 p.m. Tours at the winery, 3 miles away, are by appointment.

This winery features handcrafted premium wines, including Cabernet Sauvignon, Chardonnay, Sauvignon Blanc, Zinfandel, Merlot and Muscat. The vineyards were planted between 1981 and 1983, and the first wine was released in 1984. The grounds are attractively landscaped, and there is a small patio for picnicking.

MOSBY WINERY AT VEGA VINEYARDS
Off US 101 at 9496 Santa Rosa Rd., Buellton (mailing address: P.O. Box 1849, 93427). (805) 688-2415. Open for tasting daily 10 a.m. to 4 p.m. $2.50 tasting fee. Tours by appointment only.

Bill and Jeri Mosby planted their vineyard on what was once part of the Rancho de la Vega, a 19th-century land grant. They converted the old carriage house into a winery and in 1979 crushed their first vintage there. Today the Mosby family produces wine from estate-grown and purchased grapes. Varieties include not only Chardonnay, Gewürztraminer and Pinot Noir, but also the Italian varieties—Sangiovese, Nebbiolo, Primativo and Pinot Gris. Visitors are welcome to picnic.

NORMAN VINEYARDS, INC.
4 miles off SR 46 W. at 7450 Vineyard Dr., Paso Robles, 93446. (805) 237-0138; FAX (805) 227-6733. Open for tasting Sat., Sun. and holidays 11 a.m. to 5:30 p.m., or by appointment. Additional tasting Mon. through Sat. 10 a.m. to 5 p.m. at Adelaida Floral, 300 Main St., Templeton. (805) 434-2997.

The owner's ancestors have been involved in viticulture and winemaking since the 15th century on the slopes of Lake Geneva in Switzerland; in the late 19th century they carried their wine legacy to Northern California. The winery was founded in 1971 and is nestled amid the vineyards. Wines are handcrafted, and production of Zinfandel, Cabernet Sauvignon, Chardonnay, White Zinfandel,

Cabernet Franc and No Nonsense Red is 3000 cases a year. The large outdoor patio area complements the old Spanish winery building and overlooks the vineyards, gardens and a brook flowing through an area of oaks, mulberry and toyon. Picnic facilities are available.

OLD CREEK RANCH WINERY
1½ miles south of Oak View at the end of Old Creek Rd. (mailing address: P.O. Box 173, 93022). (805) 649-4132. Open for tasting Fri. through Sun. 10 a.m. to 4 p.m. Tours by appointment.

Established in 1981, Old Creek Ranch lies along the banks of San Antonio Creek in the southern end of the Ojai Valley. Grapes from Santa Maria Valley and Ventura County produce six types of varietal wine.

PESENTI WINERY
3 miles west of Templeton at 2900 Vineyard Dr., 93465. Phone and FAX (805) 434-1030. Open for tasting Mon. through Sat. 8 a.m. to 6 p.m., Sun. from 9 a.m.

In 1923 Frank and Caterina Pesenti planted the original Zinfandel vines;

these are dry-farmed, which means that the vines are non-irrigated and survive on soil moisture. The winery was built in 1934 and is still operated by the Pesenti family. Specialties include Zinfandel, Cabernet Sauvignon and several varieties of white wines. Over the years Pesenti has garnished its share of prestigious awards. There is a gift shop for visitors.

RANCHO SISQUOC WINERY
18 miles southeast of Santa Maria via US 101 at Betteravia and 6600 Foxen Canyon Rd., 93454. (805) 934-4332. Open for tasting and tours daily 10 a.m.to 4 p.m.

Rancho Sisquoc is a large cattle ranch near the Sisquoc River in the foothills of the San Rafael Mountains. The entrance to the ranch is marked by the San Ramon Chapel; cattle and quail can be seen along the drive that winds its way to the winery. A small portion of the ranch has been planted to grapes, with the first crush in 1972. Commercial winemaking began in 1977 when the winery was bonded; now 8000 cases of varietal wines are bottled each year. Beautiful picnic grounds are adjacent to the charming, rustic tasting room.

The historical architecture of Norman Vineyards blends with its setting.

Norman Vineyards

ROSS-KELLER WINERY
985 Orchard Ave., Nipomo 93444. (805) 929-3627. Open for tasting and tours daily noon to 5 p.m.

Ross-Keller's owners are horse breeders, and the winery is family operated on their Standardbred Ranch. Ross-Keller's goal is to produce as natural a product as possible; locally grown, purchased grapes are vinified with almost no processing or additives. Annual production is 3000 cases per year of red and white varietals. Visitors are welcome to use the winery's picnic area.

SANFORD WINERY
5 miles west of US 101 at 7250 Santa Rosa Rd., Buellton 93427. (805) 688-3300; FAX (805) 688-7381. Open for tasting daily 11 a.m. to 4 p.m.

Richard and Thekla Sanford produce 36,000 cases annually of Chardonnay, Pinot Noir, Sauvignon Blanc and Pinot Noir-Vin Gris. There are picnic facilities adjacent to the winery.

SANTA BARBARA WINERY
202 Anacapa St., Santa Barbara 93101. (805) 963-3633, (800) 225-3633; FAX (805) 962-4981. Open for tasting daily 10 a.m. to 5 p.m. Tours daily at 11:30 a.m., 3:30 p.m. and by appointment.

Santa Barbara Winery was established by Pierre LaFond in 1962, making it both the oldest producing winery in Santa Barbara County and the first since prohibition. Although they began by purchasing their grapes, 10 years later they planted their own 72 acres in the Santa Ynez Valley. Winemaker Bruce

McGuire believes that what happens in the field is what makes for the quality and integrity of the wines. He uses the ancient practice of whole-cluster fermentation, which brings out the spicy, intense fruit flavors of the grape and the finish tannins in the wine. Production also includes Chardonnay, barrel-fermented dry Chenin Blanc, Johannisberg, Paradis (dry White Riesling), White Zinfandel, Cabernet Sauvignon, Sauvignon Blanc and a late harvest wine.

SANTA YNEZ WINERY
343 N. Refugio Rd., Santa Ynez 93460. (805) 688-8381; FAX (805) 688-3764. Open for tasting and self-guided tours daily 10 a.m. to 5 p.m. Guided tours by appointment only. Three other tasting rooms (no tours) are located at:

Copenhagen Cellars, *448 Alisal Rd., Solvang 93463. (805) 688-4218. Open daily 11 a.m. to 6 p.m., Nov. to Feb. to 5 p.m.*

Historic Stearns Wharf, *217-G Stearns Wharf, Santa Barbara 93101. (805) 966-6624. Open daily 9 a.m. to 9 p.m., Nov. to Feb. to 6 p.m.*

Winemaker Bruce McGuire blends Chardonnay at Santa Barbara Winery.

Ventura Harbor Village, *1591 Spinnaker Dr., Ventura 93001. (805) 644-WINE. Open daily 11 a.m. to 6 p.m., Nov. to Feb. to 5 p.m.*

The Old College Ranch was dairy land for over 50 years, until three resident Santa Ynez families, the Giffords, the Davidges and the Bettencourts, joined forces to plant the first commercial vineyards in 1969. The first crush yielded 500 cases in 1979. Now the remodeled barn is used to make 18,000 cases of wine annually. Emphasis is on white varietals, including Sauvignon Blanc, Chardonnay and Riesling, all from the winery's 110-acre vineyard. Picnic facilities are available, and from July through September the winery sponsors a series of three twilight dinners (reservations are necessary). The Solvang location has unique Danish fruit wine tasting. See Annual Events section for the Santa Ynez and Ventura location events.

SILVER HORSE VINEYARDS
East off US 46 at 2995 Pleasant Rd., San Miguel 93451 (mailing address: P.O. Box 2010, Paso Robles 93447). (805) 467-WINE. Open for tasting and self-guided tours Mon. through Thur. 11 a.m. to 5 p.m. Closed Tue. and Wed.

Rich Simons makes wine and Kristen Simons raises Thoroughbreds on their 44 acres. The winery produces 3500 cases of Cabernet Sauvignon, Zinfandel, Chardonnay, Pinot Noir and White Zinfandel. Visitors may browse the gift shop, purchase refrigerated deli items and picnic near a pond. They may also have a chance to see newborn Thoroughbreds destined for the racetrack.

TALLEY VINEYARDS
North of Orcutt Rd. at 3031 Lopez Dr., Arroyo Grande 93420. (805) 489-0446. Open for tasting 10:30 a.m. to 4:30 p.m.; Jun. through Sep. daily, and Oct. through May Mon. through Thur. Tours by appointment.

Oliver Talley began growing specialty vegetables in the Arroyo Grande Valley in the late 1940s. In 1982, the Talley family moved into viticulture and planted a test plot that has since evolved into 102 acres in three separate vineyards. The new winery was completed in 1991; production is 5000 cases per year of Sauvignon Blanc, White Riesling and the winery's specialties, Chardonnay and Pinot Noir. Visitors may sample the wines in the Rincon Adobe, built in the 1860s. A wide lawn, a gazebo, and several large round picnic tables are available to visitors.

TOBIN JAMES CELLARS
8 miles east of Paso Robles on SR 46 at 8950 Union Rd., 93446. (805) 239-2204. Open for tasting and self-guided tours daily 10 a.m. to 6 p.m. Guided tours are by appointment.

Since its first vintage in 1987, the winery now produces 6000 cases of Chardonnay, Merlot, Cabernet Sauvignon, Pinot Noir, Zinfandels, Syrah and others. A historical "10-mile-stop" building, an underground barrel room and a saloon-style tasting room with a 100-year-old bar may be of interest to visitors. A gift shop, art gallery and picnic area are also available.

TWIN HILLS WINERY
At Mustard Creek Rd. and 2025 Nacimiento Lake Dr., Paso Robles 93446. (805) 238-9148. Open for tasting Apr. through Sep., daily 10 a.m. to 6 p.m.; Nov. through Feb. call for hours. Closed Dec 25.

Caroline Scott began winemaking in her garage 12 years ago. When she met Glen Reid seven years later, she indoctrinated him into the art, and their passion for winemaking evolved into the dream of owning a winery; Twin Hills is the realization of their goal. The owners' philosophy is to minimize the use of chemicals in the farming and winemaking process. The production of natural wines includes Chardonnay, Cabernet Sauvignon, Zinfandel, California Beaujolais, Rose, White Zinfandel and the pride and joy of Twin Hills Winery, California Dry Sherry, made from Palomino grapes using an ancient "solera" technique. The spacious tasting room is styled in French Country decor and has couches and a fireplace. Picnic facilities, a gift shop and an art gallery are available to visitors.

WILD HORSE WINERY

2½ miles south of Vineyard Dr. off Templeton Rd. in Templeton (mailing address: P.O. Box 910, 93465). (805) 434-2541. Open for tasting daily 11 a.m. to 5 p.m. Closed major holidays.

Ken Volk, winemaker and owner, is also a horticulturist. He tried his hand at home winemaking in 1978, and has been making wine ever since. The French Country-style winery produces about 30,000 cases annually of Chardonnay, Pinot Noir, Merlot, Cabernet Sauvignon and about 20 other wines from its 64 acres of estate grapes and other central coast grapes. It also offers rare, exotic varietals available only in their tasting room. In 1990 Wild Horse Winery was named "Winery of the Year" by *Wine and Spirits* magazine, and in 1992 Ken Volk was named "Winemaker of the Year" by the Central Coast Winegrowers Association.

YORK MOUNTAIN WINERY

9 miles west of Templeton via SR 46 at 7505 York Mountain Rd. (mailing address: Rt. 2, Box 191, 93465). (805) 238-3925. Open for tasting daily 10 a.m. to 5 p.m. Tours by appointment only. Closed major holidays.

In 1882, after retiring from more than 61 years in the winemaking business, Max Goldman established a winery. Pinot Noir, Chardonnay, Cabernet Sauvignon and Zinfandel are vinified from the winery's 11 acres, as well as Merlot, sherry, sparkling wine and generic wine. The original winery building houses the tasting room.

ZACA MESA WINERY

15 miles north of Buellton via US 101 and Zaca Station Rd. on Foxen Canyon Rd. (mailing address: P.O. Box 899, Los Olivos 93441). (805) 688-3310. Open for tasting daily 10 a.m. to 4 p.m. Tours every hour on the half hour.

In 1973 Zaca Mesa Ranch converted 160 acres of grazing land to vineyard. A new winery was finished in time for the 1978 harvest. Now 213 acres of vineyards produce the fruit for 36,000 cases of wine each year. Zaca Mesa offers estate-bottled Chardonnay, Pinot Noir and Syrah. A gift shop and a shaded picnic area are available to visitors. Two nature trails in the foothills offer views of the nearby mountains and Foxen Canyon.

ANNUAL EVENTS

Exact dates, prices and other information about the events listed below may be verified by calling the telephone numbers shown. In addition, some wineries individually sponsor special brunches, dinners and summer concerts; for information on events sponsored by a particular winery, call that winery and ask if a calendar of events is available.

JANUARY—

WINTER BARREL TASTING
Leeward Winery, Ventura. (805) 656-5054. Free.

This two-day event features tasting of barrel samples and current releases by candlelight in the winery cellar.

FEBRUARY—

VALENTINE BLACK TIE DINNER
Eberle Winery, Paso Robles.
(805) 238-9607. Admission $85.

A romantic dinner with wine is prepared by a selected chef.

MARCH—

ZINFANDEL WEEKEND
Various locations, Paso Robles.
(805) 239-8463 (Paso Robles Vintner's
& Growers Association). Admission $35
for seminar and tasting; $55 for
celebration at wineries.

Zinfandel seminar and tasting, a charity wine auction and various events with wine, food and entertainment at participating wineries are the components of this three-day event.

APRIL—

SANTA BARBARA COUNTY VINTNERS' FESTIVAL
Flag is Up Farms, Buellton (mailing
address for tickets: Vintners' Association,
P.O. Box 1558, Santa Ynez 93460).
(805) 218-0881. Admission $55 (prices
may vary). Reservations required.

Area wineries host special events and winemaker dinners featuring 30 chefs and caterers. The weekend includes entertainment as well as food and wine tasting.

SANTA YNEZ VALLEY CARRIAGE CLASSIC
Firestone Winery meadow, Los Olivos.
(805) 688-4454, 688-3940.
Admission $10 for all three days.

This three-day event features an equestrian show and competition, food booths, music, carriage rides, trade fair, a children's section and picnic facilities.

SPRING OPEN HOUSE
Leeward Winery, Ventura.
(805) 656-5054. Free admission.

All wines are opened for tasting with appetizers in this two-day event.

MAY—

PASO ROBLES WINE FESTIVAL WEEKEND
Various locations, Paso Robles.
(805) 239-8463 (Paso Robles Vintner's
& Grower's Association). Admission
$15; includes souvenir glass and tasting
tickets.

Local wine industry leaders take to the links in a golf tournament benefiting viticultural research. Other festivities in this two-day event include jazz bands, food and tasting of over 100 wines; participating wineries schedule demonstrations, seminars and other festivities. Winemaker dinners require separate reservations and tickets.

JUNE—

OJAI WINE FESTIVAL
Special event area, Lake Casitas
(mailing address: Ojai Wine Festival,
P.O. Box 1320, Oak View 93022).
(800) 648-4881 (tickets), (805) 646-
5747. One-day admission $18, includes
souvenir glass and tasting tickets;
$10 admission without tasting for ages
12 to 20.

Local restaurants, wineries, cooking demonstrations, a barbecue, educational seminars, arts and crafts and live music are part of this one-day festival sponsored by the Rotary Club of Ojai as fund raiser to benefit various charities.

JULY—

INDEPENDENCE DAY BARBECUE
Santa Ynez Winery, Santa Ynez.
(805) 688-8381. Admission $15.

Wine tasting, a barbecue, music and games for the kids are included in this one-day event held at the winery's picnic area, which has a panoramic view of the Santa Ynez Valley.

KCBX CENTRAL COAST WINE CLASSIC
Various locations in San Luis Obispo and Santa Barbara counties (mailing address: KCBX 4100 Vachell Ln., San Luis Obispo 93401). (805) 781-3026. Admission price varies.

This five-day event features wine and wine barrel tasting, dinners at various restaurants and wineries, an auction, and brunch and dinner at Hearst Castle.

MID-SUMMER BARBECUE
Santa Ynez Winery, Ventura Harbor Village; 1591 Spinnaker Dr., Ventura. (805) 644-WINE. Admission $25.

This one-day wine tasting event is accompanied by a barbecue. It is held on the patio overlooking Ventura Harbor.

OLD FASHIONED 4TH OF JULY
Fess Parker Winery, Los Olivos. (800) 841-1104.

Vignettes recreated from history are dramatically presented in period costume. This is a one-day outdoor event with food concessions; wine is sold by the glass.

TWILIGHT DINNER SERIES #1
Santa Ynez Winery, Santa Ynez. (805) 864-3443. Admission $50.

The first of three twilight dinners features fine cuisine, special wines, barrel samples and live music.

AUGUST—

A TASTE OF VENTURA OPEN HOUSE
Leeward Winery, Ventura. (805) 656-5054. Admission free.

All wines are opened for tasting and a chef prepares food products grown locally for this two-day event.

MID-SUMMER FOOD & WINE EXPOSITION
Hope Farms Winery, Paso Robles.

(805) 238-6979. Admission $15 includes cooking class and wine glass.

This afternoon event offers a cooking class, samples of gourmet food and wine tasting.

MUSEUM WINE FESTIVAL
Santa Barbara Museum of Natural History, 2559 Puesta del Sol Rd. (805) 682-4711. Admission $35 for nonmembers; $30 for members.

This afternoon event takes place on museum grounds; oaks and sycamores along Mission Creek provide shade for the setting. Featured are the latest and best offerings from 20 county wineries paired with delicacies from 15 caterers and restaurants, and accompanied by live music. Ample parking.

TWILIGHT DINNER SERIES #2
Santa Ynez Winery, Santa Ynez. (805) 864-3443. Admission $50.

The second of three twilight dinners features fine cuisine, special wines, barrel samples and live music.

SEPTEMBER—

CENTRAL COAST WINE FESTIVAL
Mission Plaza, San Luis Obispo. (805) 546-4231 (24-hour hotline), (805) 541-1721. Admission $25.

Sponsored by the Arthritis Foundation, this event features a live band, food booths, wine tasting, wine-related items and information. Over 50 wineries participate in the event.

SWORDFISH FEAST
Santa Ynez Winery, Ventura Harbor Village. 1591 Spinnaker Dr., Ventura. (805) 644-WINE. Admission $35.

Wine tasting is accompanied by a swordfish barbecue.

TWILIGHT DINNER SERIES #3
Santa Ynez Winery, Santa Ynez. (805) 864-3443. Admission $50.

The third of three twilight dinners features fine cuisine, special wines, barrel samples and live music.

VINE TO WINE HARVEST PARTY

Santa Ynez Winery, Santa Ynez.
(805) 688-8381. Admission $25, age 10 and under free.

The afternoon celebration includes a barbecue, wine tasting, a grape stomp, music and guided tours with the winemaker.

OCTOBER—

A CELEBRATION OF HARVEST

Santa Barbara County Vintners' Association, P.O. Box 1558, Santa Ynez 93460.
(805) 688-0881. Admission price varies.

This is a one-day celebration with the county's vintners, farmers and ranchers. Musical entertainment, wine and food tasting and a variety of produce from throughout the county are featured.

CELEBRATION OF HARVEST OPEN HOUSE

Carey Cellars, Solvang.
(805) 688-8554. Admission free.

Hors d'oeuvres, wine futures and barrel tasting are featured at this event.

FESTA DELL' UVA

Various wineries along the Foxen Canyon Wine Trail.
(800) 841-1104 (Fess Parker Winery, Los Olivos). Admission free.

Held along the Foxen Canyon Wine Trail in conjunction with Celebration of Harvest, there is progressive wine tasting with different events at each winery.

HARVEST DINNER

Eberle Winery, Paso Robles.
(805) 238-9607. Admission $75.

A dinner specially prepared by a selected chef is with paired wine in celebration of harvest time.

HARVEST WINE FAIR & COUNTRY HARVEST TOUR

Hope Farms, Meridien Vineyards and the public library in Paso Robles.
(805) 239-VINE (Paso Robles Vintners & Growers Association). All-day pass purchased before Oct. 1, $50; after Oct. 1, $55.

This two-day event features gourmet foods, seminars on wine and chocolate, and the pairing of food and wine and wine tasting, as well as special events at the participating wineries.

MORRO BAY HARBOR FESTIVAL

Morro Bay Harbor.
(805) 772-1155; (800) 633-3063. Admission $3 for adults; age 11 and under free. Additional fees: $2 per seafood plate, $8 for six wine tastings with a glass and $5 for five beer tastings. Free parking and shuttles.

During National Seafood Month the California Seafood Council and the Central Coast Winegrower's Association sponsor this festival featuring samples of more than 100 wines and cuisine from over 20 seafood restaurants. The two-day event also includes a marine life exhibit, beer tasting, a tugboat regatta, ship tours, sand sculptures, a Hawaiian shirt contest, arts and crafts, live music and entertainment, Kid's Cove & Treasure Isle, and many other events.

NOVEMBER—

BEAUJOUR CELEBRATION

Santa Barbara Winery, Santa Barbara.
(805) 963-3633, (800) 255-3633. Admission $15, includes a souvenir glass.

A celebration of the first wine of harvest includes wine tasting, food and music.

EBERLE WINERY SCHOLARSHIP DINNER

Eberle Winery, Paso Robles.
(805) 238-9607. Admission $95.

This charity dinner prepared by selected chefs raises funds for promising students in the Wine Marketing Department of Cal Poly San Luis Obispo.

FALL HOLIDAY OPEN HOUSE
Leeward Winery, Ventura.
(805) 656-5054. Admission free.

All wines are opened for tasting with appetizers in this two-day event.

HARVEST CELEBRATION
Edna Valley & Arroyo Grande Valley Vintners Association. (805) 541-5868. Admission $40.

The Arroyo Grande-Edna Valley appellations hold an annual one-day celebration of wine tasting. The 20 wineries will also feature older "library" vintages and wine from barrels. Food, live music, a silent auction and vineyard tours are offered, and some wineries will host special events.

DECEMBER—

BLACK TIE CHRISTMAS GALA
Justin Vineyards, Paso Robles.
(805) 238-6932.Admission $75.

A locally known chef prepares a special dinner paired with wine for this event.

CHRISTMAS GET TOGETHER
Santa Ynez Winery, Santa Ynez.
(805) 688-8381. Admission free.

The winery presents a day of special tastings, Christmas music, appetizers and spiced holiday wine.

CHRISTMAS OPEN HOUSE
Mosby Winery at Vega Vineyards, Buellton. (805) 688-2415. Admission free.

Wine tasting, food sampling and Christmas carols make this a festive one-day holiday event.

HOLIDAY BLACK TIE DINNER
Eberle Winery, Paso Robles.
(805) 238-9607. Admission $80.

A holiday dinner is prepared by a well-known chef.

HOLIDAY OPEN HOUSE
Eberle Winery, Paso Robles.
(805) 238-9607. Admission free.

Eberle celebrates the season in their new wine caves with a day of holiday music, appetizers and tasting of special wine releases.

HOLIDAY OPEN HOUSE AT THE PASO ROBLES WINE TASTING ROOMS
Various locations, Paso Robles.
(805) 239-VINE (Paso Robles Vintners & Growers Association). Admission free. Minimal tasting fees $1-2.

Holiday-decorated wineries host open houses each in their own ways—winetasting and appetizers, hayrides and trolley rides, holiday music, wine and wine-related gifts for purchase at special prices. The chamber of commerce hosts a parade highlighting the Victorian homes on historic Vine Street.

NEW YEAR'S EVE BLACK TIE CHAMPAGNE EXTRAVAGANZA
Justin Vineyards, Paso Robles.
(805) 238-6932. Admission $75.

This is a multicourse dinner event featuring a mystery chef and matching of champagnes and foods from around the world. Music and dancing round out the evening.

Monterey to San Francisco Bay Area

Encompassed in the Monterey to San Francisco Bay Area are the wine grape growing districts of Alameda, Monterey, San Benito, San Mateo, Santa Clara and Santa Cruz counties. Much of the region has climatic features similar to those of the Russian River area. Sunny valleys are cooled by fog and coastal air currents, providing good conditions for premium wine grapes.

To the South, Monterey and San Benito counties have small wineries that are open to the public, and several large wine producers have vineyards in the area. Paul Masson and Mirassou bought acreage between Soledad and Greenfield in 1960. Since then, Almadén and others have followed suit, and vineyards now carpet much of the central and southern Salinas Valley. Nearby is Northern California's oldest wine district, the Santa Clara Valley. Here the Franciscans planted vineyards at Mission Santa Clara de Asis in 1777, nearly a half century before they introduced wine growing to the Sonoma Valley. In recent years, Santa Clara vineyards have been threatened by smog and urban sprawl, forcing many valley wineries to look elsewhere for land.

Another old viticultural area is Santa Cruz County, which supported nearly 40 wineries before Prohibition. As interest in this region has revived, many of the old wineries have been reopened by new owners, and others have been newly constructed. Most of these are small family enterprises, taking advantage of the mountain terrain and coastal climate to make high quality wines.

On the San Francisco peninsula, the hills of San Mateo County are home to several small wineries, some of which are open to the public. Although the weather is favorable for premium grapes, high land values preclude the development of large commercial vineyards.

In Alameda County, the gravelly soil of the Livermore Valley is best suited to white wine grapes, although red varieties fare well too. Petite Sirah was pioneered here by Concannon, one of the area's most familiar names. Another well-known Livermore winery is Wente Bros., whose reputation rests largely on white varietal wines.

OF SPECIAL INTEREST

A TASTE OF MONTEREY

1 block from the Monterey Bay Aquarium at 7100 Cannery Row, Monterey 93940. (408) 646-5446. Open daily 11 a.m. to 6 p.m.

This visitor center specializes in Monterey County wine and produce. In addition to wine by the glass, they offer wine tasting and sales from 23 Monterey wineries, gourmet foods and spices, educational films, and exhibits–one of which is a display of wine labels. A 20-foot mural shows the locations of

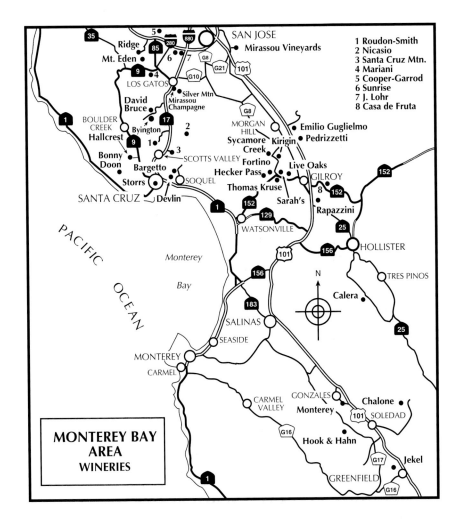

	1 Roudon-Smith
	2 Nicasio
	3 Santa Cruz Mtn.
	4 Mariani
	5 Cooper-Garrod
	6 Sunrise
	7 J. Lohr
	8 Casa de Fruta

MONTEREY BAY AREA WINERIES

wineries and vineyards. The center also has a spectacular view of Monterey Bay and across to Santa Cruz.

WINERIES IN THE MONTEREY TO SAN FRANCISCO BAY AREA

BARGETTO WINERY
3535 N. Main St., Soquel 95073; tasting room at 700 Cannery Row, Monterey.

(408) 475-2258 (winery); (408) 373-4053 (Monterey tasting room). Open for tasting daily 9 a.m. to 5 p.m. Tours Mon. through Fri. by appointment at 11 a.m. and 2 p.m. Monterey tasting room open daily 10 a.m. to 6 p.m.

The Bargettos established their family operated, coastal winery in 1933. Located along Soquel Creek, Bargetto Winery produces Santa Cruz Mountains wines and unique fruit wines, including Mead, Olallieberry,

SAN FRANCISCO
BAY AREA
WINERIES

1 Retzlaff
2 Concannon
3 Stony Ridge
4 Murietta's Well
5 Livermore Valley
6 Chouinard
7 Sunrise
8 Weibel

SEE
MONTEREY BAY
AREA MAP

TO WENTE BROS. &
CEDAR MTN.

Raspberry and Apricot. The Bargetto wines are served in the rustic tasting room and on the outdoor patio overlooking the creek, and there are refrigerated deli items for sale and a gift shop. (See also Annual Events.)

BONNY DOON VINEYARD

12 miles north of Santa Cruz via SR 1 and Bonny Doon Rd. at 10 Pine Flat Rd. (mailing address: P.O. Box 8376, 95061). (408) 425-3625. Open for tasting; May 15 through Sep. 14, daily noon to 5 p.m.; Sep. 15 through May 14, Wed. through Mon. noon to 5 p.m. Closed major holidays. Tours by appointment.

In 1983 philosophy major Randall Grahm became a viticulturalist and winemaker. He opened his small winery in a bucolic setting four miles from the ocean in the Santa Cruz Mountains, concentrating on wines made from the prominent grape varieties of France's Rhône and Provence regions and the Italian varieties. Bonny Doon currently produces premium varietal wines and eclectic blends from estate-grown and purchased fruit. Visitors are welcome to picnic under the redwoods.

BYINGTON WINERY & VINEYARDS, INC.
Off SR 17 at 21850 Bear Creek Rd., Los Gatos 95030. (408) 354-1111, ext. 204. Open for tasting daily 11 a.m. to 5 p.m. Tours by appointment.

Byington's majestic Italian-style chateau rises out of the redwoods and vineyards of the Santa Cruz Mountains. Winemaker Alan Phillips vinifies Sauvignon Blanc, Chardonnay, Cabernet Sauvignon, Pinot Noir, Merlot and Zinfandel from estate and purchased fruit. Annual production of 10,000 cases is distributed through the tasting room and by mail order. The 2000-foot elevation provides a spectacular view of Monterey Bay. Visitors may use the picnic facilities.

CADENASSO WINERY
4144 Abernathy Rd., Suisun City 94585. (707) 425-5845, 425-5845. Open for tasting Tue. through Sun. 8:30 a.m. to 5:30 p.m. Closed Jan. 1, Easter, Thanksgiving and Dec. 25.

Founded in 1906 by Giovanni Cadenasso, the winery is now headed by grandson John F. Cadenasso. Production is 9000 to 15,000 cases annually of various dry wines.

CALERA WINE CO.
11 miles south of Hollister at 11300 Cienega Rd., 95023. (408) 637-9170. Open by appointment for tours and sales.

Josh Jensen had worked in the vineyards of Burgundy, and when he came to California his search for similar limestone-rich soil ended here, on the site of an abandoned limestone quarry. Construction began in 1977 on Calera's gravity-flow winery, which spans six levels on a hillside in the Gavilan Mountains. Calera's six vineyards all lie within the Mount Harlan appellation defined in 1990. The winery makes three varietals: Chardonnay, Pinot Noir and a small amount of Viognier.

CASA DE FRUTA ORCHARD RESORT
13 miles east of Gilroy or 28 miles west of SR 5 at 10031 Pacheco Pass Hwy. (SR 152), Hollister 95023. (408) 842-9316. Open for tasting daily; Nov. to Feb. 9 a.m. to 6 p.m., Jun. through Aug. 8 a.m. to 7 p.m. Closed Dec. 25.

In the 1940s three teenaged brothers, Italian immigrants, opened a cherry stand on the Pacheco Pass Highway. From this evolved the current resort complex and winery, still operated by the Zanger family. The original fruit stand, wine tasting room, deli, country store, gas station, petting zoo, candy factory, bakery, restaurant, orchard operation (cherries, prunes, apricots, walnuts and asparagus) and a two-mile narrow-gauge railway that winds through the resort are all part of this huge complex. Wines produced are white, red, blush, champagne and gourmet fruit wines. There are ample picnic grounds for visitors; parking facilities for vehicles and RVs are available.

CEDAR MOUNTAIN WINERY
4 miles southeast of downtown Livermore at 7000 Tesla Rd., 94550. (510) 373-6636, (510) 449-9215. Open for tasting and tours Sat., Sun. and holidays noon to 4 p.m. or by appointment.

In 1988 Linda and Earl Ault purchased a four-year-old Chenin Blanc vineyard and grafted it to Chardonnay and Cabernet Sauvignon. They now produce about 1500 cases per year. The works of local artists (including Ault) are displayed in the tasting room. Picnic facilities are available. Call for monthly events.

CHALONE VINEYARD
7 miles east of Soledad off Stonewall Canyon Rd. (mailing address: P.O. Box

855, 93960). (408) 678-1717. Open for
tasting Sat. and Sun. 11:30 a.m. to 4
p.m.; open for tasting and tours by
appointment Mon. through Fri. Closed
Jan. 1, Easter, 3rd Sat. in May,
Thanksgiving and Dec. 25.

Chalone is situated at an elevation of
2000 feet in the Gavilan Mountains.
This is the oldest producing vineyard in
Monterey County, established by
Frenchman Curtis Tamm, who was
looking for soil similar to the chalky soil
of his native Burgundy. It has been
planted to grapes in the "Cote d' Or of
Burgundy" tradition since 1919, with
subsequent plantings in later years.
Annual production is about 35,000
cases of Chardonnay, Pinot Noir,
Chenin Blanc and Pinot Blanc. Picnic
facilities and gift items are available.
The property is within 2½ miles of the
Pinnacles National Monument.

CHOUINARD VINEYARDS
*33853 Palomares Rd., Castro Valley
94552. (510) 582-9900; FAX (510)
733-6274. Open for tasting and tours Sat.
and Sun. noon to 5 p.m. and some holidays.*

This small, family operated winery is set
in picturesque Palomares Canyon. Built
in 1925, the winery produces 4500 cases
of Chardonnay, Zinfandel, Johannisberg
Riesling, Cabernet Sauvignon, Petite
Sirah, Gewürztraminer, Sparkling Wine
and Granny Smith Apple Wine. There
are hiking trails, a gift shop, picnic
facilities and wildflower walks. Call the
winery about wine, nature and music
events in the vineyards.

CONCANNON VINEYARD
*2 miles southeast of Livermore at 4590
Tesla Rd. (Co. Rd. J2), 94550. (510)
447-3760. Open for tasting and tours daily
10 a.m. to 4:30 p.m., Sat. and Sun. from
11 a.m. Horse carriage tours of the vineyard are offered Sat. and Sun. from noon
to 3 p.m. and Mon. through Fri. by
appointment.*

James Concannon founded Concannon
Vineyard in 1883. Then, as today,
Concannon's focus is on growing the
highest quality grapes to make the finest
wine. The vineyard's gravelly soil
proved ideal for producing grapes with
refined, subtle flavors. Concannon used
the gravel to its advantage, pioneering
the first Petite Sirah in 1961. In 1994,
the winery won more than 100 awards
for wines such as their Cabernet
Sauvignon, Petite Sirah, Chardonnay
and Sauvignon Blanc. As a result,
Concannon was named as one of the
top 10 wineries in America. Visitors are
welcome to picnic.

COOPER-GARROD ESTATE VINEYARDS
*22600 Mt. Eden Rd, Saratoga 95070.
(408) 867-3335. Open for tasting Sat.
and Sun. 11 a.m. to 4:30 p.m. Call for
holiday schedule.*

Vineyard master Jan Garrod's great-
grandfather purchased this agricultural
land in 1893. This family operated
winery and 21-acre estate now produce
2500 cases of Chardonnay, Cabernet
Franc and Cabernet Sauvignon. The
wine tasting room was a fruit-storage
building built in 1922. There are gift
wine items for sale and a picnic area.

DAVID BRUCE WINERY
*5 miles southwest of Los Gatos at 21439
Bear Creek Rd., 95030. (408) 354-4214.
Open for tasting daily noon to 5 p.m.
Closed Thanksgiving and Dec. 25.*

Nestled high in the Santa Cruz Mountains amid redwoods and vineyards, the
winery is the creation of Dr. David
Bruce, a dermatologist and wine
enthusiast. In 1961, influenced by fine
wines produced from Santa Cruz Mountain grapes by the legendary Martin Ray,
Bruce purchased 40 acres near Los
Gatos. A gifted innovator, his use of and
experimentation in various winemaking
techniques have culminated in a

reputation for classically styled premium wines: Chardonnay, Pinot Noir and Cabernet Sauvignon. Annual production is 25,000 cases. Visitors may use the picnic area.

DEVLIN WINE CELLARS

Off SR 1, exit Park Ave. east to 3801 Park Ave., Soquel (mailing address: P.O. Box 728, 95073). (408) 476-7288; FAX (408) 479-9043. Open for tasting Sat. and Sun. noon to 5 p.m. Tours by appointment.

Founded in 1978, winemaker Charles Devlin produces 10,000 cases a year of Chardonnay, Merlot and champagne. Visitors can tour the gardens and picnic with a view of Monterey Bay.

EMILIO GUGLIELMO WINERY

1480 E. Main Ave., Morgan Hill 95037. (408) 779-2145. Open Mon. through Fri. 9 a.m. to 5 p.m., Sat. and Sun. from 10 a.m. Closed major holidays. Tours for groups of 20 or more by appointment only.

The Guglielmo name has been synonymous with winemaking for centuries, tracing back to the hilly Piedmont winegrowing region of northern Italy. Emilio Guglielmo arrived in the Santa Clara Valley in 1908, and 17 years later established a winery. His simple philosophy has been carried on through the generations—producing natural, quality wines to share with family and friends. Today, more than 100,000 gallons of varietals are produced annually. A concert area and picnic facilities are available to visitors; gift and deli items are available for purchase. Dinner events featuring notable chefs are offered four times per year; call for details. (See also Annual Events.)

FENESTRA WINERY

1 mile west of SR 84 and Holmes St./Wetmore Rd. at 83 Vallecitos Rd., Livermore 94550 (mailing address: P.O.

Box 582, Sunol 94586). (510) 447-5246, 862-2292; FAX (510) 862-2283. Open for tasting Sat. and Sun. noon to 5 p.m. Closed Jan. 1, Easter, Thanksgiving and Dec. 25.

Built in 1889 by pioneer viticulturist George True, the 8000-square-foot winery building has been refurbished with a new roof, hundreds of French and American oak barrels and stainless steel tanks. Winemaker Dr. Lanny Replogle, a chemistry professor now retired from San Jose State University, and his wife Fran produce a wide range of premium varietal wines: Cabernet Sauvignon, Cabernet Franc, Pinot Noir, Merlot, Zinfandel, Sémillon, Semmonay (a Sem-Chard) and a sweet dessert wine. Also produced is True Red, named after George True, a blend of Pinot Noir, Zinfandel and Merlot. There are picnic facilities for visitors.

FORTINO WINERY

5 miles west of Gilroy off SR 152 at 4525 Hecker Pass Hwy., 95020. (408) 842-3305, 847-0387; FAX (408) 842-8636. Open for tasting and tours daily 10 a.m. to 5 p.m. Closed Jan. 1, Easter, Thanksgiving and Dec. 25.

In 1970 Ernest Fortino purchased the Cassa Brothers' Winery and converted production from bulk to varietal wines. Production includes four white wines, six red wines and two champagnes. Dessert wines include raspberry, olallieberry, apricot and mead wines. A picnic area, a European boutique and a gift, gourmet and deli shop are available for visitors. Some featured specialty items are Raspberry Chardonnay Fudge, Chocolate Cabernet Fudge, and dressings or mayonnaise made with Garlic Pinot or Sauvignon. Refrigerated picnic items are sold.

HALLCREST VINEYARDS

6 miles north of Santa Cruz at 379 Felton-Empire Rd., Felton 95018. (408) 335-

4441. *Open for tasting daily 11 a.m. to 5:30 p.m. Tours by appointment.*

The original Hallcrest Vineyards were founded in 1941 by Chafee Hall, and the last Hallcrest label vintage was pressed in 1964, when Hall retired. Several wineries maintained the vineyards after his death in 1968. Felton-Empire Vineyards reopened the site in the late 1970s, and in 1987 the Schumacher family bought the property, restoring its original name. Now Hallcrest produces about 15,000 cases per year of varietal wines and grape juices. The winery is also the second-largest producer of organic wines in the United States, bottled under the Organic Wine Works label. A picturesque picnic area overlooks the vineyards. (See Annual Events.)

HECKER PASS WINERY
5 miles west of Gilroy at 4605 Hecker Pass Hwy., 95020. (408) 842-8755. Open for tasting daily 10 a.m. to 5 p.m. Tours by appointment.

Established in 1972, the winery naturally ferments its wines in redwood tanks and matures them in small oak barrels, oak casks and redwood tanks. The vineyards supply all the grapes for the premium varietals made and sold under the Hecker Pass label. There is a selection of dry table wines, as well as sherries and ports. The rustic tasting room has a 20-foot redwood bar that overlooks the vineyard and picnic areas.

J. LOHR WINERY
1000 Lenzen Ave., San Jose 95126. (408) 288-5057. Open for tasting daily 10 a.m. to 5 p.m. Tours Sat. and Sun. at 11 a.m. and 2 p.m.

Jerry Lohr's winery produced its first wines in 1974 from their downtown facility. Estate-owned vineyards are located in Monterey County and Paso Robles. Production is about 350,000 cases annually, and current offerings include Cabernet Sauvignon, Chardonnay, Gamay, Johannisberg Riesling, Merlot, Fumé Blanc and White Zinfandel.

JEKEL VINEYARDS
1 mile west of US 101 at 40155 Walnut Ave., Greenfield (mailing address: P.O. Box 336, 93927). (408) 674-5525. Open for tasting daily 10 a.m. to 5 p.m. Tours by appointment.

The Jekel family planted 140 acres of vineyards in 1972 and an additional 190 acres a decade later in the Arroyo Seco district of the Salinas Valley. Now owned by Brown-Forman, the ultra-modern winery produces 60,000 cases of premium varietals each year; the wines are made from grapes grown in the winery's vineyards, which are planted to Cabernet Franc, Cabernet Sauvignon, Chardonnay, Pinot Noir and Riesling.

KIRIGIN CELLARS
5 miles west of Gilroy via SR 152 and Co. Rd. G8 at 11550 Watsonville Rd., 95020. (408) 847-8827. Open for tasting daily; Jun. through Aug. 10 a.m. to 6 p.m., Sep. through May to 5 p.m. Tours by appointment.

Historic Solis Rancho was situated in the "Uvas" Valley, named by Spaniards who found wild grapes growing here. Acquired in 1976 by Nikola Kirigin-Chargin, it was renamed Kirigin Cellars. Part of the existing building, a landmark in the area, dates back to 1827 and it is still in use as the family residence. Nikola Kirigin-Chargin has a degree in enology from the University of Zagreb and is a distinguished winemaker.

LIVE OAKS WINERY
4 miles west of Gilroy at 3875 Hecker Pass Hwy., 95020. (408) 842-2401. Open for tasting daily 10 a.m. to 5 p.m. Closed Jan. 1, Easter, Thanksgiving, and Dec. 25.

Founded in 1912 by Eduardo Scagliotti, the winery is now operated by Peter

Scagliotti, Eduardo's youngest son. Annual production is 4000 cases of Chenin Blanc, Burgundy, Chardonnay, Gewürztraminer, Johannisberg Riesling, Zinfandel, White Zinfandel, Sauvignon Blanc and Sweet Johannisberg Riesling. The winery specializes in premium quality burgundy, aged in redwood tanks for longer than 65 months. Before the winery's land was cleared it was heavily wooded with oak trees; some that remain are more than 350 years old. The winery displays and sells celebrity photos; a gift shop and picnic area are available for visitors.

LIVERMORE VALLEY CELLARS

1 mile south of Livermore off SR 84 at 1508 Wetmore Rd., 94550. (510) 447-1751. Open for tasting and tours daily 11:30 a.m. to 5 p.m.

This small winery, built in 1978, is located in an insulated metal building and is seemingly on the verge of being overwhelmed by suburban housing tracts. The Lagiss family produces wine from estate-grown grapes; their 34-acre vineyard is planted to Grey Riesling, Chardonnay, Golden Chasselas, French Colombard and Servant Blanc. The yield ranges from 1000 to 3000 cases per year, with fruit purchased from other vineyards during drought years. There are picnic facilities and a park nearby.

MARIANI WINERY AND SARATOGA VINEYARDS

At SR 9 and Big Basin Rd.; 23600 Congress Springs Rd., Saratoga
95070. (408) 741-2930. Open for tasting daily 11 a.m. to 5 p.m. Tours by appointment.

Nestled in the redwoods along the historic "Chaine D' Or" (Golden Chain) in the Santa Cruz Mountains, Mariani Vineyards was established by French immigrant Pierre Pourroy in 1892; wines are still made from some of the original plantings. Production includes Cabernet Franc, Carignane, Zinfandel and Chardonnay. The historic Villa de Monmartre sits atop a vine-covered hill and is used for special events. The winery's 1912 redwood tasting room also has a gift shop and a working cellar.

MIRASSOU CHAMPAGNE CELLARS

½ mile off Main St. at 300 College Ave., Los Gatos 95032. (408) 395-3790. Open for tasting and tours Wed. through Sun. noon to 5 p.m.

The fourth generation of Mirassous, Edmund and Norbert, produced

Mariani Winery is set in a seemingly enchanted circle surrounded by a redwood forest in the Santa Cruz Mountains' "Chaine d' Or" (Golden Chain).

49

Mirassou's first bottling of *méthode champenoise* sparkling wine in 1954 to celebrate the 100th anniversary of family winemaking. Today, the sparkling wines are made at the old Novitiate Winery in the foothills above Los Gatos, where the Jesuits produced wines from 1888 to 1985.

MIRASSOU VINEYARDS
1½ miles east of Capitol Expy. at 3000 Aborn Rd., San Jose 95135. (408) 274-4000; FAX (408) 270-5881. Open for tasting and tours Mon. through Sat. noon to 5 p.m., Sun. to 4 p.m.

Mirassou family tradition holds that when Pierre Pellier ran out of water for his vine cuttings on the ship from Europe to America, he bought a shipment of potatoes on board and planted his cuttings in the potatoes for moisture. He built his winery in 1860, six years after planting his first vineyards, and in 1881 his oldest daughter married Pierre Mirassou. Now in its fifth generation of family ownership, brothers Daniel, Jim and Peter Mirassou produce a number of vintage-dated varietal wines at their San Jose facility. (See Annual Events.)

THE MONTEREY VINEYARD
West of US 101 at 800 S. Alta St., Gonzales (mailing address: P.O. Box 780, 93901). (408) 675-2316. Open for tasting daily 10 a.m. to 5 p.m. Tours at 11 a.m., 1 and 3 p.m. Closed major holidays.

The Monterey Vineyard is a picturesque example of Mexican-Spanish architecture; it is graced with ornamental ironwork and 25-foot stained glass windows depicting the many different grape varietals. The winery produces five varietal wines from grapes grown in Monterey County. An art gallery features rotating exhibits of works by local artists. The gift shop carries refrigerated deli items

and large variety of wine-related gift items; there is a picnic area with ducks and a gazebo.

MOUNT EDEN VINEYARDS
22020 Mt. Eden Rd., Saratoga 95070. (408) 867-5832; FAX (408) 867-4329. Open for tasting and tours by appointment.

Mount Eden is a small winery located at an elevation of 2000 feet in the Santa Cruz Mountains. From vines first planted by Martin Ray in the 1940s and from nonestate Chardonnay grapes purchased from the MacGregor Vineyards in Edna Valley, the winery produces a few thousand cases of Chardonnay, Cabernet Sauvignon and Pinot Noir. In 1991, construction was completed on a 4000-square-foot cave. Arrangements to visit the winery should be made at least a week in advance.

MURRIETA'S WELL
¼ mile south of Tesla and Mines rds. at 3005 Mines Rd., Livermore 94550. (510) 449-9229. Open for tasting and tours; Mon. through Fri. by appointment, Sat. and Sun. 11 a.m. to 4:30 p.m. $5 tasting fee.

Legendary outlaw Joaquin Murrieta often used a well that lies on the winery's property, hence its name. Built in the 1890s, the winery calls up images both of the romance of wine and the heyday of the ranchos. In the 1980s restoration of the structure began, and it opened to the public in 1992. Antique winemaking equipment and old photographs line the upstairs walls, and sit-down tastings are done at tables made from old barrels topped with glass. The winery is a joint venture between winemaker Sergio Traverso and Philip Wente. Production focuses on two proprietary blends (currently the winery's only national releases), and two styles of Chardonnay and a Zinfandel which are available only at the winery.

NICASIO VINEYARDS

483 Nicasio Wy., Soquel 95073. (408) 423-1073. Open for tasting and tours by appointment.

This small winery produces varietals and Naturelle Champagne; its first vintage was in 1952. Picnic facilities are available for visitors.

OBESTER WINERY

2 miles east of Half Moon Bay at 12341 San Mateo Rd. (SR 92), 94019. (415) 726-9463. Open for tasting daily 10 a.m. to 5 p.m.

Situated in a picturesque valley surrounded by flower fields, pumpkin patches and Christmas tree farms, Obester makes premium wines and gourmet food products. A second winery is located in the Anderson Valley.

PAGE MILL WINERY

13686 Page Mill Rd., Los Altos Hills 94022. (415) 948-0958. Open for tasting and tours by appointment.

Dick Stark's basement winery saw its first crush of 1000 gallons in 1976. With his whole family assisting, production tripled the next year and has now leveled off at 2500 cases annually. Four varietal table wines are made from purchased grapes. Because the winery is part of the Stark residence, appointments to visit the winery are essential.

PEDRIZZETTI WINERY

1 mile east of Morgan Hill off US 101 via Dunne and Murphy aves. at 1645 San Pedro Ave., 95037. (408) 779-7389. Open for tasting daily 10 a.m. to 5 p.m. Tours by appointment.

The Pedrizzettis bought their winery in 1945. Their enterprise has been based on table wines, notably Barbera (renowned for 46 years) and White Zinfandel. Production also includes dessert, aperitif and sparkling varieties. Visitors are welcome to picnic; there are facilities for up to 160 people.

RAPAZZINI WINERY

3 miles south of Gilroy on US 101 (mailing address: P.O. Box 247, 95020). (408) 842-5649; Garlic Shoppe (408) 848-3646. Open for tasting daily; Jun. through Aug. 9 a.m. to 6 p.m., Sep. through May, Mon. through Fri. to 5 p.m., Sat. and Sun. to 6 p.m.

Established in 1962, the winery was destroyed by fire in 1980. Rebuilt in 1982, the beautiful tasting room has a 40-foot-long copper bar and the Garlic Shoppe sells gift and gourmet items. Rapazzini produces premium varietal and specialty wines.

RETZLAFF VINEYARDS

2 miles south of downtown Livermore at 1356 S. Livermore Ave., 94550. (510) 447-8941. Open for tasting Mon. through Fri. noon to 2 p.m., Sat. and Sun. to 5 p.m. $3 tasting fee refundable with purchase.

In a green barn behind an 1885 farmhouse, Bob and Gloria Taylor vinify Cabernet Sauvignon, Chardonnay, Grey Riesling, Merlot, Sauvignon Blanc and a Meritage blend from their 14 acres of vineyards. The former sheep ranch was planted to grapes in 1977, the first vintage was crushed in 1986, and annual production now stands at 3000 cases per year. Retzlaff Vineyards is the closest winery to downtown Livermore, and the expansive shaded picnic area is a popular lunchtime destination for tourists and local business people. The winery also hosts a series of "Full Moon Dinners" from late spring to early autumn.

RIDGE VINEYARDS

7 miles northwest of I-280 at 17100 Monte Bello Rd., Cupertino 95014. (408) 867-3233. Open for tasting Sat. and Sun. by appointment.

Since 1962, Ridge has championed single-vineyard winemaking, exploring California in search of great vineyards where climate, soil and varietal are perfectly matched. Ridge uses traditional methods and minimal handling to produce their wines.

ROSENBLUM CELLARS

Opposite the Alameda Naval Air Station at 2900 Main St., Alameda 94501. (510) 865-7007; FAX (510) 865-9225. Open for tasting and tours Mon. through Fri. 10 a.m. to 5 p.m., Sat. and Sun. from noon.

California's only "island winery" is housed in a spacious former locomotive repair barn. Winemaker Kent Rosenblum purchases grapes from older and hillside dry-farmed vineyards in Napa and Sonoma counties. The winery specializes in Zinfandel, Cabernet Sauvignon, Merlot and Petite Sirah, and it produces small quantities of white varietal wines and a *méthode champenoise* sparkling Gewürztraminer. Call to request newsletter. (See Annual Events.)

ROUDON-SMITH VINEYARDS

2 miles north of Scotts Valley Dr. at 2364 Bean Creek Rd., Santa Cruz 95066. (408) 438-1244. Open for tasting and tours Sat. 11 a.m. to 4:30 p.m., Sun. by appointment.

A pair of former engineers made the first Roudon-Smith wines in the Santa Cruz Mountains in 1972. The winery moved to its present rustic location in 1978, and production is now 10,000 cases per year. Attention is focused on a few premium varietals, with an emphasis on Santa Cruz Mountains Estate Chardonnay, and on Cabernet Sauvignon, Petite Sirah, Merlot and Zinfandel, vinified from grapes grown in various California coastal regions.

SANTA CRUZ MOUNTAIN VINEYARD

2300 Jarvis Rd., Santa Cruz 95065. (408) 426-6209. Open for tasting and tours by appointment.

Ken Burnap founded his winery in 1974, and has since expanded his original Pinot Noir production to include Chardonnay, Merlot and Cabernet Sauvignon. The four varietals account for the compact winery's total output of 3000 cases per year. Traditional methods are used to vinify grapes grown in unirrigated mountain vineyards. Visitors with appointments follow a narrow, scenic mountain road to the winery.

SARAH'S VINEYARD

5 miles west at 4005 Hecker Pass Hwy., Gilroy 95020. (408) 842-4278. Open for tasting and tours by appointment.

This small winery is located in a shaded redwood building on a hillside overlooking a 13-acre Chardonnay vineyard, an apple orchard and rolling hills. Winemaker Marilyn Sarah Clark produces about 2000 cases annually of Chardonnay and red table wine from estate and purchased grapes.

SILVER MOUNTAIN VINEYARDS

Call for directions to location (mailing address: P.O. Box 3636, Santa Cruz 95063). (408) 353-2278. Open for tasting and tours by appointment.

Jerold O'Brien, a retired military pilot, embraced the myriad difficulties of mountain vineyard farming here in the Santa Cruz Mountains. Founded in 1979, the original winery and cellar were destroyed in the 1989 Loma Prieta earthquake, but O'Brien saw it as an opportunity to start over and create better facilities. Production is currently about 1700 cases per year, and will increase with the completion of new facilities. Ten acres of vineyards lie adjacent to the winery. Visitors receive a tour of the chateau-like winery and are invited to stroll the grounds and decks, which offer spectacular views of the mountains and Monterey Bay.

O'Brien makes Chardonnay, Zinfandel and Merlot in a French Bordeaux style.

SMITH & HOOK AND HAHN ESTATES
4 miles north of Soledad off US 101 via Arroyo Seco Rd. at 37700 Foothill Rd. (mailing address: P.O. Drawer C, 93960). (408) 678-2132. Open for tasting and tours daily 11 a.m. to 4 p.m.

The winery and vineyards at Smith & Hook are perched high above the Salinas Valley on the steep eastern slope of the Santa Lucia Mountains. The 250 acres of estate vineyards produce 50,000 cases per year of Cabernet Sauvignon. Cabernet has been the winery's specialty since its first vintage in 1979, and winemaker Duane DeBoer has been with the winery since before the vineyard was planted. The winery is housed in a 28,000-gallon refurbished redwood tank. Guests are welcome to use the picnic area.

SOLIS WINERY
3 miles west of Gilroy on SR 152 at 3920 Hecker Pass Hwy., 95020. (408) 847-6306; FAX (408) 847-5188. Open for tasting Wed. through Sun. 11 a.m. to 5 p.m. Tours by appointment. Tasting fee.

Solis is a family operated winery on 12 acres, producing Merlot and Chardonnay. There are picnic facilities for visitors, as well as a gift shop and an art gallery.

STONY RIDGE WINERY
2½ miles southeast of downtown Livermore at 4948 Tesla Rd., 94550. (510) 449-0458; FAX (510) 449-0646. Open for tasting Mon. through Sat. 11 a.m. to 5 p.m., Sun. noon to 5 p.m. Tours by appointment. Restaurant open Mon. through Sat. 11 a.m. to 2 p.m.

Carrying a deep appreciation for the history of the Livermore Valley and for her own family history, Monica Scotto bought the Stony Ridge Winery in

1985 and, along with her family, began working to restore the brand's former prestige. Annual production consists of 20,000 cases per year of seven varietal and two blended wines, all available for tasting. The tasting bar, once part of their father's Pleasanton winery, runs along one side of the tasting room, which shares space with Scotto's restaurant. A large redwood deck fronts the structure and provides a place for outdoor dining in the summer.

STORRS WINERY
½ mile south of SR 1 off River St. exit at Old Sash Mill; 303 Potrero St., Santa Cruz 95060. (408) 458-5030; FAX (408) 458-0464. Open for tasting and tours Fri. through Mon., noon to 5 p.m.

In 1988 Stephen and Pamela Storrs founded Storrs Winery, located in the Old Sash Mill in Santa Cruz. Their winery is one of only a handful operated by a husband and wife enology team. Using traditional winemaking methods, they are dedicated to the production of four Chardonnays from the cool mountain vineyards of the Santa Cruz Mountains. They also vinify Gewürztraminer, Zinfandel and Merlot. Their selection of low-tonnage, coastal-area vines produces enough fruit for about 4000 cases per year.

SUNRISE WINERY
Off I-280 at 13100 Montebello Rd., Cupertino 95014. (408) 741-1310; FAX (408) 741-1310. Open for tasting Fri. through Sun. 11 a.m. to 3 p.m.

This 1880s winery ranch is listed on the National Register of Historic Places. Located on a 350-acre wildlife preserve, the winery produces 2500 cases of Chardonnay, Pinot Blanc, Estate Zinfandel, Pinot Noir and Cabernet Sauvignon. A gift shop and areas for walking and picnicking are available for visitors.

SYCAMORE CREEK VINEYARDS
4 miles west of Morgan Hill at 12775 Uvas Rd., 95037. (408) 779-4738, 779-5873. Open for tasting Sat. and Sun. 11:30 a.m. to 5 p.m.

Early explorers found California's native vines growing abundantly in this valley. Built in 1906 and named Marchetti Ranch, this family vineyard was eventually closed during Prohibition. It was acquired in 1975 by former schoolteachers Terry and Mary Kay Parks, who renamed it Sycamore Creek. It was the first generation of super-premium producers in an area traditionally known for its reasonably priced jug wines. Their wines now have a long list of medals and awards. In 1989 the Parks sold the winery to Kazuaki Morita; the winery now exports part of its production to Japan. Production includes estate-grown Chardonnay and Cabernet Sauvignon; other select vineyards provide fruit for Johannisberg Riesling and Gamay Blanc.

THOMAS KRUSE WINERY
5 miles west of Gilroy at 4390 Hecker Pass Hwy., 95020. (408) 842-7016. Open for tasting and tours (maximum 5 people) daily noon to 5 p.m. Closed major holidays.

In 1971 Tom Kruse launched his two-man operation, one of the smallest wineries in Santa Clara County with only one acre of vineyards. The wine list includes a number of dry varietal table wines, plus two bottle-fermented sparkling wines.

WEIBEL VINEYARDS
1 mile south of Mission San Jose via SR 238 at 1250 Stanford Ave. (mailing address: P.O. Box 3398, 94539). (510) 656-2340. Open for tasting daily 10 a.m. to 5 p.m. 10-minute guided tours Mon. through Fri until 3 p.m.

The Weibel vineyards were originally the domain of Leland Stanford, who founded his winery in 1869. The winery has been named a historical landmark and since 1945 has been owned by the Weibel family. There is a tasting room set amidst a grove of trees, with a picnic area adjacent.

WENTE BROS. ESTATE WINERY
2 miles southeast of Livermore at 5565 Tesla Rd., 94550. (510) 447-3603. Open for tasting Mon. through Sat. 10 a.m. to 4:30 p.m., Sun. from 11 a.m. Tours Mon. through Sat. at 10 and 11 a.m. and 1, 2 and 3 p.m.; Sun. at 1, 2 and 3 p.m. Tasting and tours (same hours) are also available at Wente Bros. Sparkling Wine Cellars, 5050 Arroyo Rd. (510) 447-3694; restaurant (510) 447-3696.

The fourth generation of Wentes now oversees the winery launched by Carl Wente in 1883. From 48 acres, the Wente family operations have grown to include nearly 2000 acres of vineyards, two historic wineries and a cattle ranch. The Wente brothers introduced the first California wines to be labeled Chardonnay, Sauvignon Blanc and Sémillon. Production is centered in the Livermore Valley, where guides give a thorough tour of the facility. The other location, Wente Bros. Sparkling Wine Cellars, is a restored old winery with deep sandstone caves for bottle-aging and has a restaurant.

WOODSIDE VINEYARDS
340 Kings Mountain Rd., Woodside 94062-3618. (415) 851-3144. Open for tasting and tours Sat. and Sun. by appointment.

Woodside Vineyards was founded in 1960 when the owners built a wine cellar under their carport. Two of the 20 acres of vines are gnarled stock from the old, previously abandoned La Questa vineyards. Woodside wines, which include Cabernet Sauvignon, Pinot Noir, Zinfandel and Chardonnay, are available in extremely limited quantities.

ANNUAL EVENTS

Exact dates, prices and other information about the events listed below may be verified by calling the telephone numbers shown. In addition, some wineries individually sponsor special brunches, dinners and summer concerts; for information on events sponsored by a particular winery, call that winery and ask if a calendar of events is available.

MARCH—

MONTEREY WINE FESTIVAL
Marriott Hotel and Monterey Conference Center, Monterey.
(800) 656-4282 (Monterey Wine Festival). Call for admission and event prices.

This four-day festival includes wine tasting, culinary arts, tours of historic sites, tastings, dinners and lunches, educational programs, a golf tournament and more. A wine auction features oversize and unusual bottles; proceeds benefit scholarships.

APRIL—

SPRING WINE FESTIVAL
Casa de Fruta County Park, Santa Clara.
(800) 548-3813 (Casa de Fruta); (408) 779-2145 or 778-1555 (Santa Clara Valley Winegrower's Association). Admission $25.

The day's events include a steak dinner with wine, music and dancing.

WINERY OPEN HOUSE
Rosenblum Cellars, Alameda.
(510) 865-7007. Admission $6.

Wine tasting of future barrels and current bottles, live music and light food are part of this two-day open house.

MAY—

BLUEGRASS ARTS AND WINE FESTIVAL
Hallcrest Vineyards, Felton.
(408) 335-4441. Admission $12.50 per day.

Several live bands, arts and crafts booths and wine tasting are featured at this two-day festival.

MORGAN HILL MUSHROOM MARDI GRAS
Morgan Hill.
(408) 779-9444 (Morgan Hill Chamber of Commerce). Admission $6.

This two-day festival includes food, arts and crafts booths, a wine tent, three stages with continuous entertainment and a children's area with games, rides and shows.

JUNE—

CRAFTS IN THE COURTYARD
Bargetto Winery, Soquel.
(408) 475-2258. Admission free.

This event features two days of wine tasting and crafts.

LA DOLCE VITA
Guglielmo Winery, Morgan Hill.
(408) 779-2145. Admission $25 including food, wine tasting and raffle.

This festival features a day of live music, food, wine and a raffle.

VINTNERS' FESTIVAL
Various locations in Santa Cruz, San Mateo and Santa Clara counties. (mailing address: Santa Cruz Mountains Winegrowers Association, P.O. Box 3000, Santa Cruz, 95063).
(408) 479-9463 (479-WINE). Admission $15, includes a commemorative glass that serves as a ticket to each participating winery.

Two "passport weekends" featuring annual open houses at the wineries (some usually not open to the public) are held with different special events planned at each location. Events include vertical and library tastings, special vintages, art shows, cooking demonstrations and music.

JULY—

JAZZ AND WINE CELEBRATION
Mirassou Vineyards, San Jose.
(408) 274-4000. Admission $24.

The day's activities feature three jazz bands, a gourmet barbecue lunch and wine tasting.

WEARABLE ART SHOW
Bargetto Winery, Soquel.
(408) 475-2258. Admission free.

Wine tastings and original handmade wearable art are the focus of this two-day show.

AUGUST—

ARTISTS WEEKEND, OUTDOOR FESTIVAL OF FINE ART
Bargetto Winery, Soquel.
(408) 475-2258. Admission free. $3.50 wine tasting fee includes glass. Food sampling fee.

Over a two-day period, 30 local artists display their work in front of the winery. Featured are paintings, prints, sculpture, photography, bonsai, music, food booths and wine tasting.

HARVEST BARBECUE
Guglielmo Winery, Morgan Hill.
(408) 779-2145. Admission $25.

A steak barbecue, music, games and raffles are the features of this one-day, family oriented event.

WINEMAKERS' CELEBRATION
Custom House Plaza at Fisherman's Wharf, Monterey.
(408) 375-9400. Admission $10 in advance, $15 at the door; includes a glass and 5 tasting tickets. Fee for food sampling.

This one-day celebration features a showcase for regional foods and wines as well as music, educational displays, barrel-building demonstrations, grapevine pruning and corking discussions.

WINERY OPEN HOUSE
Rosenblum Cellars, Alameda.
(510) 865-7007. Admission $6.

Wine tasting of future barrels and current bottles, live music and light food are part of this two-day open house.

SEPTEMBER—

CAPITOLA ART & WINE FESTIVAL
The Esplanade, Capitola Village.
(408) 475-6522 (Capitola Chamber of Commerce). Admission free. Wine tasting is $6 for commemorative glass and $1 per tasting ticket.

This two-day event features sampling booths from local wineries and restaurants, more than 150 arts and crafts booths, live entertainment including bluegrass, jazz, swing, folk, and classical music, and performances by theater and dance groups. The children's area has food, entertainment and participatory art booths.

SANTA CLARA ART & WINE FESTIVAL
Central Park, 969 Kiely Blvd., Santa Clara.
(408) 984-3257 (City of Santa Clara Parks & Rec. Dept.). Admission free. Fees for wine and food sampling.

The day's activities include crafts, food and wine booths, live entertainment and a children's area with crafts and games.

OCTOBER—

FALL HARVEST WINE FESTIVAL
Casa de Fruta County Park, Santa Clara.
(800) 548-3813 (Casa de Fruta); (408) 779-2145, 778-1555 (Santa Clara Valley Winegrower's Association). Admission $22.

This one-day event includes appetizers with wine, music and dancing.

NOVEMBER—

HOLIDAY FESTIVAL
*Mirassou Vineyards, San Jose.
(408) 274-4000. Admission $7 including commemorative glass. Food sampling fee.*

This two-day, Dickens-theme festival features strolling carolers, jazz musicians, a barbershop quartet, wine tasting, food booths from local restaurants and hot mulled wine.

WINERY OPEN HOUSE
*Rosenblum Cellars, Alameda.
(510) 865-7007. Admission $6.*

Wine tasting of future barrels, current bottles, live music and light food takes place over two days.

DECEMBER—

CHRISTMAS GIFT FAIR
*Guglielmo Winery, Morgan Hill.
(408) 779-2145. Admission free.*

Boutique gift packs made especially for the holidays are sold during the two-day fair. Champagne, cheese and crackers are served with wine tasting.

CHRISTMAS WINE TRAILS
*14 wineries in Livermore Valley.
(510) 447-9463 (Livermore Valley Wine Growers). Admission free.*

Decorated for the holidays, the wineries host two days of wine tasting before Christmas, with holiday music and arts and crafts.

HOLIDAY ART IN THE WINE CELLARS
*Bargetto Winery, Soquel.
(408) 475-2258. Admission free. $3.50 tasting fee includes souvenir glass. Food sampling fee.*

More than 20 local artists display their work in the winery cellars, accompanied by holiday music and food samples during this two-day event.

WINERY OPEN HOUSE
*Smith & Hook and Hahn Estates, Soledad.
(408) 678-2132. Admission free.*

All wines are poured for tasting during this one-day open house. Sale items include cheese and wine cakes as well as holiday gifts.

Napa, Sonoma, Mendocino and Lake Counties

The **Napa** and **Sonoma** valleys are the best known of California's wine districts. Divided by the Mayacamas mountain range, they have similar weather conditions, with sunny days tempered by cooling marine breezes and fog. These conditions are best for premium grape varieties such as Cabernet Sauvignon, Pinot Noir and Chardonnay.

In 1769 the Franciscan fathers began winemaking at their first mission in San Diego. By 1823 the Franciscan fathers' mission trail ended in Sonoma, where they planted more vineyards for making church wine. In the 1830s the missions were secularized and fell into neglect, along with the vineyards. During that same decade, California's Mexican governor, General Mariano Guadalupe Vallejo, came to Sonoma and revived the mission vineyards. In the 1850s Hungarian adventurer Count Agoston Haraszthy arrived in the area, and consequently founded Buena Vista Winery—the oldest winery in California today. In 1861 he brought back cuttings from Europe and planted over 300 European varieties of vines, propelling California's wine industry into a new era. Also located in the Sonoma valley is Jack London State Historic Park, named after the writer who made the area famous in his 1913 novel, *The Valley of the Moon.* Sonoma Valley, Sonoma Mountain and the Carneros district (located in both Napa and Sonoma areas) are all viticultural appellations of this area.

East of Sonoma lies California's most renowned wine region—the Napa Valley. Measuring 35 miles in length and from one to four miles in width, the valley is cut through its center by the Napa River. The acclaimed "Rutherford Bench" area lies along the western side of SR 29 from Dwyer Road in the south to Grgich Hills in the north. Along the Silverado Trail, the Stags Leap district extends south from Yountville Cross Road to just beyond Clos du Val. Many Napa Valley wineries, including Charles Krug, Beaulieu and Beringer, have been producing premium wines for nearly a hundred years or more, and the wine boom of the 1980s added a host of newer names. Disasters such as phylloxera, World War II and Prohibition greatly set back winegrowing in Napa. Nevertheless, the Napa region has emerged to become a magnet for tourists. Attracted by the area's beauty and the proliferation of wineries, the summer and weekend visitor will often encounter very crowded roads and tasting rooms in the Napa Valley. For historical information on the Napa region, John Conway's *Napa* chronicles the last 20 years of drama and history in the Napa Valley, and Robert Louis Stevenson's *The Silverado Squatters* was researched and written in Napa.

Farther north, and stretching through **Mendocino** and **Lake** counties, the Russian River passes between ridges of the Coast Range. This area, with climate zones similar to the Napa Valley, has been producing wine for over a century. Wineries are scattered along most of the river's length, which parallels US 101 from

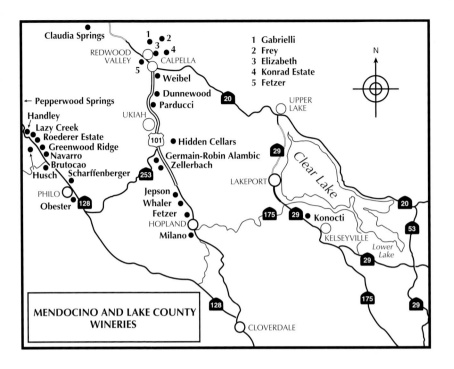

Claudia Springs

1 2
3 4
REDWOOD VALLEY
CALPELLA
5
Weibel

1 Gabrielli
2 Frey
3 Elizabeth
4 Konrad Estate
5 Fetzer

N

Dunnewood
20
Parducci
UPPER LAKE

← Pepperwood Springs
Handley
Lazy Creek
Roederer Estate
Greenwood Ridge
Navarro
Brutocao
Husch Scharffenberger

UKIAH

101

Hidden Cellars

29

Clear Lake

Germain-Robin Alambic
Zellerbach

253

LAKEPORT

PHILO
Obester
128

Jepson
Whaler
Fetzer
HOPLAND
Milano

175   29   Konocti

20

KELSEYVILLE

53

Lower Lake

29

MENDOCINO AND LAKE COUNTY
WINERIES

128

175

29

CLOVERDALE

Redwood Valley to Healdsburg and then heads west to the Pacific. More wineries are located in tributary valleys and in the Anderson Valley, a separate region that has a mild climate and high rainfall.

For many years most of the area's grapes went into bulk and jug wines, but the 1960s brought increasing interest in the potential for producing premium wines. Most wineries in the area responded to the trend and began concentrating their efforts on vintage-dated varietals.

The wine boom brought numerous newcomers to the Russian River, Dry Creek, Alexander, and the Redwood and Anderson valleys. Among them are many small wineries that devote their attention to a limited, select stock of premium varietal wines. Operating on a larger scale and for a broader market are a number of very big and impressively constructed facilities.

The Sonoma County Wine and Visitors Center, off US 101 in Rohnert Park, offers travelers video views of county scenery in addition to wine tasting, a demonstration vineyard and winery, special tours and events, and retail sales of more than 200 wines and wine-related gifts. The center is located at 5000 Roberts Lake Road via Golf Course Drive; telephone (707) 586-3795.

The Russian River Wine Road Association (707-433-6782), established in 1976, presently links more than 50 wineries in this region that welcome visitors; special directional signs are posted on local roads between Windsor and Cloverdale.

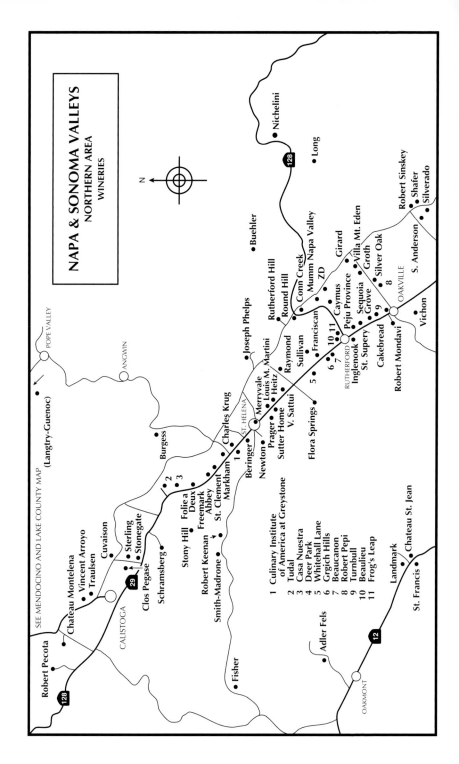

NAPA & SONOMA VALLEYS
NORTHERN AREA
WINERIES

N

Nichelini

Long

128

Buehler

Rutherford Hill
Round Hill

Conn Creek
Mumm Napa Valley
ZD

Girard
Villa Mt. Eden
Groth
Silver Oak

Robert Sinskey
Shafer
Silverado

S. Anderson

OAKVILLE

Caymus
Peju Province
Sequoia
Grove
9
St. Supery
8

Vichon

Joseph Phelps

Franciscan
10 11

Cakebread

Robert Mondavi

6 7
RUTHERFORD
Inglenook

Raymond
Sullivan
5

Merryvale
Louis M. Martini
Prager   Heitz
Sutter Home
V. Sattui

Flora Springs

Charles Krug

ST. HELENA

Beringer
Newton

Burgess

1

Markham
St. Clement

Freemark
Abbey
Folie a
Deux

2
3

Stony Hill

Robert Keenan
Smith-Madrone

POPE VALLEY

ANGWIN

(Langtry-Guenoc)

SEE MENDOCINO AND LAKE COUNTY MAP

Chateau Montelena
Vincent Arroyo
Traulsen
Cuvaison

Sterling
Stonegate

Clos Pegase

Schramsberg

CALISTOGA

Robert Pecota

128

29

1   Culinary Institute
     of America at Greystone
2   Tudal
3   Casa Nuestra
4   Deer Park
5   Whitehall Lane
6   Grgich Hills
7   Beaucanon
8   Robert Pepi
9   Turnbull
10   Beaulieu
11   Frog's Leap

Adler Fels

Landmark
Chateau St. Jean

St. Francis

12

OAKMONT

Fisher

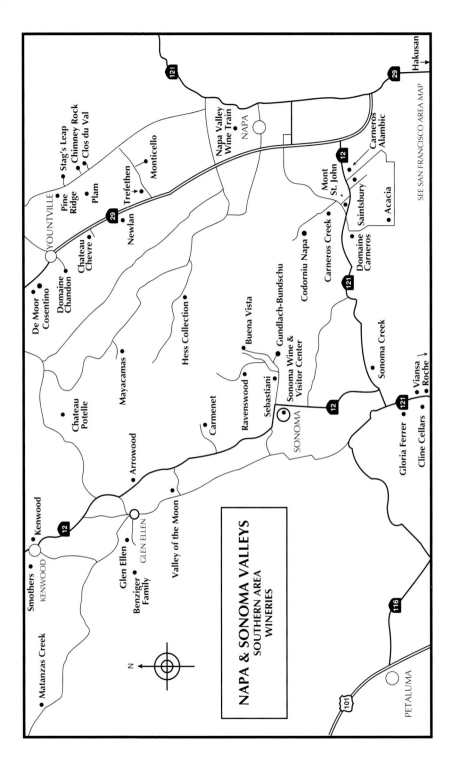

NAPA & SONOMA VALLEYS
SOUTHERN AREA WINERIES

Hakusan

SEE SAN FRANCISCO AREA MAP

NAPA

Napa Valley Wine Train

Stag's Leap
Chimney Rock
Clos du Val
Monticello

Carneros Alambic

Mont St. John

Saintsbury
Acacia

Pine Ridge
Plam
Trefethen

YOUNTVILLE
Chateau Chevre
Newlan

Carneros Creek

Domaine Carneros

Codorniu Napa

De Moor
Cosentino
Domaine Chandon

Hess Collection

Mayacamas

Buena Vista

Gundlach-Bundschu

Sonoma Creek

Chateau Potelle

Carmenet
Ravenswood
Sebastiani

Sonoma Wine & Visitor Center

SONOMA

Viansa
Roche

Arrowood

Gloria Ferrer
Cline Cellars

Kenwood

Valley of the Moon

GLEN ELLEN
Glen Ellen

Benziger Family

Smothers
KENWOOD

Matanzas Creek

N

PETALUMA

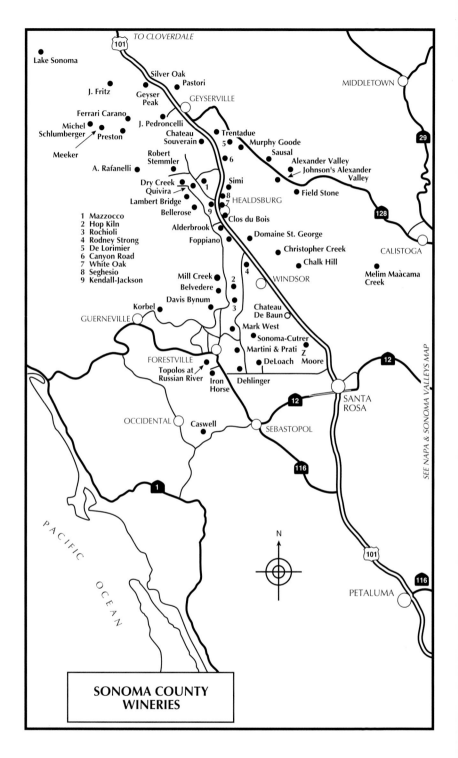

TO CLOVERDALE

101

• Lake Sonoma

• J. Fritz

Silver Oak
• Pastori

Geyser
Peak

GEYSERVILLE

MIDDLETOWN

Ferrari Carano

Michel
Schlumberger
Preston

J. Pedroncelli

Meeker

Chateau
Souverain

Trentadue

5

Murphy Goode

29

Sausal

Robert
Stemmler

6

Alexander Valley
Johnson's Alexander
Valley

• A. Rafanelli

Simi

Dry Creek
Quivira

1

• Field Stone

Lambert Bridge

8
7

HEALDSBURG

128

Bellerose

9

1 Mazzocco
2 Hop Kiln
3 Rochioli
4 Rodney Strong
5 De Lorimier
6 Canyon Road
7 White Oak
8 Seghesio
9 Kendall-Jackson

Clos du Bois

CALISTOGA

Alderbrook

Domaine St. George

Foppiano

Christopher Creek

Chalk Hill

Melim Maàcama
Creek

4

Mill Creek

2

WINDSOR

Belvedere

Davis Bynum

3

Korbel

Chateau
De Baun

GUERNEVILLE

Mark West

Sonoma-Cutrer

12

Martini & Prati

Z
Moore

FORESTVILLE

DeLoach

12

Topolos at
Russian River

Iron
Horse

Dehlinger

SANTA
ROSA

OCCIDENTAL

Caswell

SEBASTOPOL

116

PACIFIC

116

OCEAN

N

PETALUMA

101

SEE NAPA & SONOMA VALLEYS MAP

SONOMA COUNTY
WINERIES

62

OF SPECIAL INTEREST

CALISTOGA WINE STOP
1458 Lincoln Ave., #2, Calistoga.
(707) 942-5556. Open daily.

More than 1000 choices of wine from the Napa and Sonoma area are available, including half-bottles and large bottles.

CULINARY INSTITUTE OF AMERICA AT GREYSTONE
2555 Main St., St. Helena.
(707) 967-1100.

The old Christian Brothers Greystone Cellars, circa 1889, is now the country's most prestigious school for professional chefs. The school uses a two-acre organic garden, and graduates prepare Mediterranean-style lunch and dinner for patrons in the 125-seat restaurant. A museum shop of culinary artifacts, chef's supplies and cookbooks is open to the public. Call for restaurant reservations or information.

GARDENS
Many wineries have spectacular gardens that are worth a visit. **Sutter Home Winery** (707-963-3104) has hundreds of flowers encircling an 1884 Victorian home; garden plants at **Schramsberg Vineyards** (707-942-4558) date to the 1880s, and can be seen by appointment; **Traulsen Vineyards** (707-942-0283) has a large garden of roses and perenni-

als; at **Chateau Montelena** (707-942-5105) a lake with exotic pagodas can be seen on guided tours (by appointment).

HOT AIR BALLOON RIDES
(707) 944-8793.

Professional Balloon Pilots Association of Napa Valley lists companies offering flights over Napa Valley.

NAPA VALLEY WINE TRAIN
1275 McKinstry St., Napa.
(707) 253-2111, (800) 427-4124.

One way to become acquainted with the Napa area wineries is to take a three-hour, 36-mile excursion by train through the wine country. A wine-tasting car, lounge car and dining car (brunch, lunch or dinner) have been authentically and elegantly restored for the narrated, 12-mile-an-hour round trip from Napa to St. Helena.

TRIPS ON TAPE
(510) 653-2553. $12.95.

Maps from The Rider's Guide direct visitors through Napa Valley in their own vehicles.

WALKING TOURS
Napa Conference and Visitors Bureau,
1310 Napa Town Center, Napa 94559.
(707) 226-7459.

Maps for five walking tours of Napa's highlights are available for a small fee.

Visitors to Beringer Vineyards may join one of the comprehensive tours that progress from the production area to the beautiful gardens and the Rhine House.

WINERY TOURS

Winery tours vary—some provide a glimpse of the winemaking process, others include the vineyards and some even have seminars; for specific information call the winery prior to visiting. While each winery is unique, not only its products but in its setting, processes, history and other aspects, a few wineries have achieved renown among tourists: **Mumm Napa Valley** (707-942-3434) has been written up as the best for tour and tour guides; at **Beringer Vineyards** (707-963-4812) a 45-minute tour combines historical detail with a visit to their caves, which date to the 1800s; **St. Supéry Winery and Wine Discovery Center** (707-963-4507) has a self-guided tour including such elements as a relief map of the valley and its soil, and explanations of vineyard methods; **Merryvale Vineyards** (707-963-7777) offers a tour and beginner's tasting seminar on Saturday mornings for $5;

Robert Mondavi (707-226-1335) has a comprehensive, one-hour guided tour, and June through October on Tuesday evening they offer a 3½-hour tour and wine-essence tasting, sampling 24 wine-associated scents; **Domaine Chandon** (707-944-2280) demystifies the *méthode champenoise*; **Sterling Vineyards** (707-942-3344) can be accessed only by aerial tram; **Simi Winery** (707-433-6981) has a highly-praised tour; **V. Sattui** (707-963-7774) has a tour featuring its underground caves dating to the 1800s.

WINERIES IN THE NAPA, SONOMA, MENDOCINO AND LAKE COUNTIES

A. RAFANELLI WINERY
4685 W. Dry Creek Rd., Healdsburg 95448. (707) 433-1385. Open for tasting daily 10 a.m. to 4 p.m.; tours by appointment only.

The Rafanelli family has made wine in the Dry Creek Valley for three generations. They now produce 8000 cases annually (Chardonnay, Pinot Noir, Sauvignon Blanc and Zinfandel) and specialize in estate-bottled Zinfandel and Cabernet Sauvignon.

ACACIA WINERY

4 miles southwest of Napa at 2750 Las Amigas Rd., 94559. (707) 226-9991; FAX (707) 226-1685. Open for retail sales 10 a.m. to 4:30 p.m.; tasting and tours by appointment. Closed Easter.

The philosophy at Acacia Winery has not changed since it was founded in 1979: the idea was to be associated every day with something that one truly loved in life, and the answer was wine. The winery's location in the Carneros area, which is comprised mostly of grazing land and dairies, offered an opportunity to make Chardonnay and Pinot Noir. Capital to remodel the facility was provided in 1986 by the Chalone Wine Group when it acquired the winery. Acacia's wines are recognized as some of the finest from the Carneros area. The winery also produces Zinfandel and a sparkling wine.

ADLER FELS

7 miles northeast of Santa Rosa at 5325 Corrick Ln., 95409. (707) 539-3123. Tasting and tours by appointment only.

In 1980 David Coleman and Ayn Ryan built their picturesque winery, 1500 feet above the Sonoma Valley floor. They annually produce about 15,000 cases of white and red varietal table and sparkling wines. The winery's name derives from Eagle Rock, a local landmark.

ALDERBROOK WINERY

2306 Magnolia Dr., Healdsburg 95448. (707) 433-9154. Open for tasting daily 10 a.m. to 5 p.m.; tours by appointment only.

Alderbrook, owned by George and Dorothy Gillemot, has been in opera-

tion since 1981. This 63-acre ranch in the southern tip of Dry Creek Valley is planted to Zinfandel Chardonnay and Sauvignon Blanc, which make up the majority of its 30,000-case production. Alderbrook also specializes in Gewürztraminer, Merlot, Pinot Noir, Syrah and Late Harvest Muscat de Frontignan. The Hospitality Center, located in the heart of the vineyards, is surrounded by a veranda with a magnificent view of the vineyards. Visitors are invited to picnic and shop at the gift and gourmet shop.

ALEXANDER VALLEY VINEYARDS

8 miles southeast of Geyserville at 8644 SR 128, Healdsburg, 95448. (707) 433-7209. Open for tasting daily 10 a.m. to 5 p.m.; tours by appointment only.

Alexander Valley Vineyards lies alongside the Russian River. The small winery was built in 1975, and mature vineyards allowed production to begin immediately. The winery specializes in eight estate-bottled varietal wines. The winery is the setting of Cyrus Alexander's original homestead and is a Sonoma County historical landmark.

ARROWOOD VINEYARDS & WINERY

1 mile north of Madrone Rd. at 14347 Sonoma Hwy., Glen Ellen (mailing address: SR 12, P.O. Box 987, 95442). (707) 938-5170. Open for tasting daily 10 a.m. to 4:30 p.m.; tours by appointment only. Closed Jan. 1, Easter, Thanksgiving and Dec. 25.

Sixteen years after becoming Chateau St. Jean's first winemaker—and first employee—Richard Arrowood began making wine under his own name. In 1987, he and his wife Alis built their winery in the style of a New England farmhouse. Annual production is 20,000 cases of Cabernet, Chardonnay, Merlot, Viognier and a late harvest Riesling.

Michelle De Lude

The Russian River winds through Mendocino and Sonoma counties to the Pacific Ocean and helps define the Alexander, Dry Creek and Russian River appellations.

BEAUCANON WINERY

South of St. Helena on SR 29 at 1695 St. Helena Hwy., 94575. (707) 967-3520; FAX (707) 967-3527. Open for tasting daily 10 a.m. to 5 p.m.

The de Coninck family has been producing wines in France's Bordeaux region for more than 250 years. In 1987 Jacques de Coninck purchased a 65-acre property in Napa Valley, with the purpose of making wine with a French touch. The architecture of Beaucanon conveys a feeling of classic European style. The unpartitioned interior space and vaulted ceiling are similar to many wine cellars in France's Bordeaux region. Tradition and technology are the key in the winery's 30,000-case annual production of Chardonnay, Merlot, Cabernet Sauvignon and Late Harvest Chardonnay.

BEAULIEU VINEYARD

1960 St. Helena Hwy. (SR 29), Rutherford 94573. (707) 963-2411. Open for complimentary tasting and tours daily 10 a.m. to 5 p.m.; last tour at 4 p.m. Closed Jan. 1, Easter, Thanksgiving and Dec. 25.

Beaulieu Vineyard (also known simply as BV) is one of Napa Valley's oldest family wineries; it was founded in 1900 by Georges de Latour. A newly renovated visitor's center and historic tasting room are located across the parking lot from the visitors center; older vintages may be tasted for a small fee.

BELLEROSE VINEYARD

1¼ miles west of Healdsburg at 435 W. Dry Creek Rd., 95448. (707) 433-1637. Open for tasting daily 11 a.m. to 4:30 p.m.; tours by appointment only. Closed major holidays.

Bellerose Vineyard is a "chateau concept," family owned winery specializing in Bordeaux-style Cabernet, Merlot and Sauvignon Blanc.

BELVEDERE WINERY

4 miles west of Healdsburg at 4035 Westside Rd., 95448. (707) 433-8236. Open daily 10 a.m. to 4:30 p.m.

In Italian, Belvedere means "beautiful view," and a visit to the winery's deck reveals a view of picturesque vineyards in the Russian River Valley. Belvedere specializes in Chardonnay, Cabernet Sauvignon, Merlot and Zinfandel from its premium vineyards. Visitors may picnic on the sunny deck or under a shady tree, or visit the gift shop and art gallery.

BENZIGER FAMILY WINERY

1883 London Ranch Rd., Glen Ellen 95442. (707) 935-3000; FAX (707) 935-3016. Open for tasting daily 10:30 a.m. to 4:30 p.m. Tram tour at noon, 2 and 3:30 p.m. covers vine development through wine product. Closed Jan. 1, Easter, Thanksgiving and Dec. 25.

Several generations of the Benziger family worked to transform this onetime historical landmark ranch and resort into a modern wine estate. Located on the road to Jack London State Historic Park, the winery produces a large number of varietal wines, along with several proprietary wines. The pine-paneled tasting room adjoins the cellars and offers excellent views. Guests may visit The Imagery Art Gallery, purchase deli items and picnic in the redwood grove.

BERINGER VINEYARDS

2000 Main St., St. Helena 94574. (707) 963-4812. Open daily 9:30 a.m. to 5 p.m., last tour at 4 p.m. Free tasting included with tour; reserve wines can be tasted for a fee.

Established in 1876 by the Beringer brothers, this is the oldest continuously operating winery in the Napa Valley. The Beringer home, a richly decorated, 17-room mansion called the Rhine House, is listed on the National Register of Historic Places and was modeled after the family's ancestral home in Germany.

Behind it, caves carved out more than 100 years ago hold barrels of aging wine. These are viewed on informative 30-minute guided tours, which end at the tasting room in the Rhine House.

BRUTOCAO CELLARS & VINEYARDS

Tasting room at 7000 SR 128, Philo 95466. (707) 895-2152. Open for tasting daily 10 a.m. to 6 p.m.

This 500-acre vineyard produces 7500 cases of Chardonnay, Sauvignon Blanc, Sémillon, Merlot, Zinfandel, Cabernet Sauvignon and Pinot Noir. A gift shop and picnic area are open to visitors.

BUEHLER VINEYARDS

7 miles east of St. Helena off Silverado Tr. via Howell Mountain and Conn Valley rds. at 820 Greenfield Rd., 94574. (707) 963-2155. Tours Mon. through Fri. by appointment.

The stately buildings of the Buehler family winery are situated on a wooded hillside overlooking Lake Hennessey. Nearby, 61 acres of a 15-year-old vineyard yield the ingredients for 30,000 cases per year of Chardonnay, Cabernet Sauvignon, Pinot Noir and Red and White Zinfandel.

BUENA VISTA WINERY

1 mile east of Sonoma Plaza at 18000 Old Winery Rd., Sonoma (mailing address: P.O. Box 1842, 95476). (800) 926-1266. Open for tasting daily 10:30 a.m. to 4:30 p.m. Historical presentation at 2 p.m.

Agoston Haraszthy founded Buena Vista Winery in 1857. For several years it was the largest winery in the world, but then it suffered a succession of mishaps: the vines were damaged by the plant louse phylloxera, the 1906 earthquake collapsed some of the hillside tunnels, and finally the winery closed down. Today, production is carried on in a modern winery on Buena Vista's

1300-acre estate in the Carneros district. The tasting room and art gallery are in the winery's restored press house, which is a state historical landmark, and historical presentations are offered lasting 20 to 30 minutes. Visitors are welcome to picnic in the tree-shaded picnic area.

BURGESS CELLARS

5 miles northeast of St. Helena at 1108 Deer Park Rd. (mailing address: P.O. Box 282, 94574). (707) 963-4766. Open for retail sales daily 10 a.m. to 4 p.m.; tasting and tours by appointment only.

In 1972 Thomas Burgess acquired this picturesque, century-old stone winery. Its hillside location above the vineyards offers a magnificent view of the Napa Valley. Production is limited to a small selection of premium varietal table wines; the quantity is not sufficient to permit regular tasting, but by appointment visitors can arrange a tasting and tour the old cellars and the adjoining modern building.

CAKEBREAD CELLARS

1 mile south of Rutherford at 8300 St. Helena Hwy. (mailing address: SR 29, P.O. Box 216, 94573). (707) 963-5221. Open for retail sales daily 10 a.m. to 4 p.m.; tasting and tours by appointment only.

This small family winery was established in 1973. The initial redwood building and a newer barrel aging facility are bordered by 73 acres of vines. The Cakebread label appears on five varietal wines: Chardonnay, Sauvignon Blanc, Cabernet Sauvignon, Merlot and Zinfandel.

CANYON ROAD WINERY

19550 Geyserville Ave., Geyserville (mailing address: P.O. Box 25, 95441). (707) 857-3417; FAX (707) 857-3545. Open for tasting daily 10 a.m. to 5 p.m. Closed Jan. 1, Easter, Thanksgiving and Dec. 25.

Owned by Geyser Peak Winery, Canyon Road and Nervo Wines are local traditions. In production are Cabernet Sauvignon, Chardonnay, Sauvignon Blanc, Merlot and Sequoia Red. Picnic facilities are available for guests.

CARMENET VINEYARD

1700 Moon Mountain Dr., Sonoma 95476. (707) 996-5870. Tours by appointment only.

Carmenet lies nestled in a hollow in the hills above the Sonoma Valley. The winery has twin-turreted buildings of a unique conical design, in harmony with the volcanic hills surrounding it. Wines are barrel-aged in vaulted underground caverns carved into an adjacent mountainside. The hilly, 70-acre Moon Mountain estate vineyard produces Cabernet Sauvignon and other red wines; Chardonnay and Sauvignon Blanc are produced with fruit from the San Giacomo Vineyard in Sonoma County and the Paragon Vineyard in San Luis Obispo County's Edna Valley.

CARNEROS ALAMBIC BRANDY DISTILLERY

1250 Cuttings Wharf Rd., Napa Valley 94559. (707) 253-9055. Open for tasting and tours daily; Jun. through Aug. 10 a.m. to 5 p.m., Nov. through Feb. 10:30 a.m. to 4:30 p.m. $2 per-person fee for 30-minute tour.

Resembling the romantic brandy houses that dot the countryside in France's Cognac region, Carneros Alambic Distillery is both the oldest brandy distillery in America and the only one in Napa Valley. The Still House contains eight exotic, French-built copper stills which are shaped like Aladdin's Lamps. The Barrel House's nearly 4000 barrels of aging brandy produce aromas known as the "angel's share." In production are rare alembic brandies, other brandies and fine liqueurs.

CARNEROS CREEK WINERY

1285 Dealy Ln., Napa 94559. (707) 253-9463. Open for tasting daily 9 a.m. to 4:30 p.m. except major holidays. $2.50 tasting fee refundable with purchase.

In 1973, Francis Mahoney planned Carneros Creek as a small family winery built in the French style. The winery produces 20,000 cases annually. Nine acres of Pinot Noir vineyards are in production with an additional 11 planted in 1985. All wines are handcrafted by a small staff who combine California technology with old European traditional methods.

CASA NUESTRA

4 miles north of St. Helena at 3451 Silverado Tr., Napa 94559. (707) 963-5783; FAX (707) 963-3174. Open for tasting and guided tours Fri. through Sun. 11 a.m. to 5 p.m.; other times call for appointment. $2 tasting fee.

Founded in 1980 by Gene and Cody Kirkham, Casa Nuestra produces 1000 cases a year of Dry Chenin Blanc, Late Harvest Chenin Blanc, Johannisberg Riesling, Chardonnay, Italian "Field Mix" Red, Cabernet Franc and "Quixote" Meritage Blend. Visitors are welcome to use the picnic facilities.

CASWELL VINEYARDS

1½ miles east of Occidental at 13207 Dupon Rd., Sebastopol 95472. (800) 628-WINE. Open for tasting Thur. through Sat. and Mon. 10 a.m. to 5 p.m., Sun. 1 p.m. to 5 p.m.

This 12-acre vineyard produces 1500 cases of Estate Zinfandel and Chardonnay; also produced are Pinot Noir, and red and white table wines. The farm house was built in 1876. There are picnic facilities and an art gallery for visitors.

CAYMUS VINEYARDS

2½ miles east of Rutherford at 8700 Conn Creek Rd. (mailing address: P.O. Box

268, 94573). (707) 967-3011. Open for tasting daily 10 a.m. to 4:30 p.m. $2 tasting fee includes souvenir glass.

After centuries of farming in Alsace, France, the Wagner family immigrated to the Napa Valley. Since 1906, three generations of the Wagner family have farmed the area. The father and son team, Charlie and Chuck Wagner, have made Caymus Cabernet Sauvignon the hallmark of the winery. They also produce other varietals using French and American oak barrels.

CHALK HILL WINERY

10300 Chalk Hill Rd., Healdsburg 95448. (707) 838-4306. Security-gated entrance open for tasting and tours by appointment only.

Chalk Hill Winery is situated on 1100 acres owned by Frederick and Peggy Furth, and the vineyards comprise 278 acres of the estate. The area derives its name from the chalky soil in the area; the soil is made up of ash spewed out from volcanic Mount St. Helena at the northern end of the Napa Valley. The grapes for the winery's Chardonnay, Sauvignon Blanc and Cabernet Sauvignon are grown at an elevation of 200 to 600 feet.

CHARLES KRUG WINERY

2800 Main St., St. Helena 94574. (707) 963-5057. Open for tasting Mon. through Thur. 10:30 a.m. to 4:30 p.m., Sat. and Sun. 10 a.m. to 5 p.m. Tours Thur. through Tues. at 11:30 a.m., 1:30 and 3:30 p.m. $3 and $6 tasting fees with logo glass Thur. through Tues; complimentary tasting Wed.

Charles Krug founded his winery in 1861, only to have it destroyed by fire a decade later. Krug completed rebuilding in 1874; the massive stone building he constructed is still the heart of the winery. An additional bottling and warehouse facility was added by the Peter Mondavi family, who acquired the property in 1943. The Charles Krug label appears on a wide variety of wines, including Cabernet Sauvignon, Chardonnay, Chenin Blanc, Gamay Beaujolais, Pinot Noir and Sauvignon Blanc.

CHATEAU CHEVRE

1 mile south of Yountville off SR 29 at 2030 Hoffman Ln., 94599. (707) 944-2184. Tours by appointment.

Founded in 1979 on the site of a former goat ranch, the winery building originally served as the goat milking barn. The 8½-acre vineyard was planted to Merlot in 1973, and today it supplies Merlot and Chardonnay grapes for the winery's 2000 cases of wine per year.

CHATEAU DE BAUN

½ mile north of River Rd. at 5007 Fulton Rd., Fulton 95439 (mailing address: P.O. Box 11483, Santa Rosa 95406). (707) 571-7500. Open for tasting and self-guided tours daily 10 a.m. to 5 p.m.; guided tours for large groups by appointment. Closed Jan. 1, Thanksgiving and Dec. 25.

This classic French chateau is situated on 105 acres in the Russian River Valley. Annual production of 25,000 cases a year includes Champagne, Chardonnay, Pinot Noir, Symphony and Sauvignon Blanc. The impressive tasting room has a unique carved wood tasting bar; a 35-foot vaulted, beamed ceiling featuring a skylight; and a grand staircase overlooking the room. It also boasts a Louis XIV fireplace, highlighted with a soaring vertical fresco. The room's french doors and etched glass windows offer delightful views of the courtyard patio and estate vineyards. A formal rose garden, fountain, gazebos and lawn are available for visitors and picnickers. A gift shop and an art gallery are available for visitors. Summer dinner concerts are held in the Concerto Courtyard, and the Harmony Hall banquet room hosts weddings and gala affairs.

CHATEAU MONTELENA
*1429 Tubbs Ln., Calistoga 94515.
(707) 942-5105. Open for tasting daily 10
a.m. to 4 p.m.; tours by appointment daily
at 11 a.m. and 2 p.m. Closed major holidays. $5 tasting fee refundable with purchase.*

Founded in 1882, Chateau Montelena
was shut down during Prohibition and
production did not resume until 1972. In
the 1950s, former Chinese owners had
added a five-acre garden lake to the
property. The lake's two small islands
have picnic tables shaded by green-
topped pagodas and may be reserved by
visitors. The winery itself is a stone
chateau carved into a hillside. Montelena specializes in four premium quality
varietals: Chardonnay, Cabernet
Sauvignon, Zinfandel and Riesling.
Ladybugs are used as pest control each
year in the organically farmed vineyards.

CHATEAU POTELLE WINERY
*3875 Mt. Veeder Rd., Napa 94558. (707)
255-9440. Open for tasting Thur. through
Mon. 11 a.m. to 5 p.m.; tours by appointment.*

Founded in 1983, the winery produces
22,000 cases per year of Sauvignon
Blanc, Chardonnay, Cabernet
Sauvignon and Zinfandel. There is an
expansive view of the Napa Valley from
the gazebo and tasting room. Picnic
facilities are available for visitors.

CHATEAU ST. JEAN
*8 miles east of Santa Rosa at 8555 Sonoma
Hwy., Kenwood 95452. (707) 833-4134.
Open for tasting daily 10 a.m. to 4:30
p.m.; self-guided tours daily 10:30 a.m. to
4 p.m. Tasting fee for limited release and
reserve wines.*

The founders of Chateau St. Jean purchased the 250-acre estate in 1973 and
began construction of a modern winery a

Chateau St. Jean

Kenwood's charming Chateau St. Jean is reminiscent of a French Mediterranean mansion.

For Chateau Souverain, architect John Davis, who also designed Rutherford Hill Winery, blended the shape of Sonoma County's familiar hop kilns with that of a French Chateau.

year and a half later. Completed in 1980, the facility is equipped with a blend of technologically advanced equipment and traditional French oak cooperage. St. Jean's renown is built on its premium white varietals, many of which carry individual vineyard designations, and on *méthode champenoise* sparkling wines. In recent years, their red wines have also been highly acclaimed. Visitors may picnic on the grounds and taste the wines in the French Mediterranean mansion. Limited release and reserve wines are offered in the upstairs Vineyard Room.

CHATEAU SOUVERAIN

5 miles north of Healdsburg off US 101 at 400 Independence Ln., Geyserville 95441. (707) 433-3141; FAX (707) 433-5174. Open for tasting daily 10 a.m. to 5 p.m.; café open Fri., Sat. and Sun. for lunch and dinner. Closed Thanksgiving and Dec. 25.

Production includes Cabernet Sauvignon, Chardonnay, Sauvignon Blanc, Zinfandel and Merlot. There is a gift shop for visitors.

CHIMNEY ROCK WINERY

1½ miles north of Oak Knoll Ave. at 5350 Silverado Tr., Napa 94558. (707) 257-2641. Open for tasting daily 10 a.m. to 5 p.m.; tours by appointment only. Closed major holidays. $3 tasting fee includes souvenir glass or credit toward purchase.

Hack and Stella Wilson bought the Chimney Rock Golf Course in 1980, took out part of the back nine and put in grapevines, joining nine other wineries in the celebrated Stags Leap district. Production includes Fumé Blanc, Chardonnay and Cabernet Sauvignon. The winery displays a 38-foot replica of a frieze of Ganymede, cupbearer to the gods, created for the Groot Constantia Winery in Africa by sculptor Anton Anreith. A 9-hole championship golf course on the estate is open for public play.

CHRISTOPHER CREEK

2 miles southeast of Healdsburg off Old Redwood Hwy. at 641 Limerick Ln., 95448. (707) 433-2001. Open for tasting Fri. through Mon. 11 a.m. to 5 p.m., or by appointment.

Christopher Creek, formerly Rancho Sotoyome, is a small, family owned winery located southeast of Healdsburg in the rolling hills of the Russian River Valley. Using only estate-grown grapes from the 10-acre vineyard, gold medal-winning Syrah and Petite Sirah are produced in limited quantities.

CLAUDIA SPRINGS WINERY

On SR 128 between Philo and Navarro at 2160 Guntly Rd. (mailing address: P.O. Box 348, Philo 95466). (707) 895-3926, (800) 734-2160. Open for tasting and guided tours Sat. through Mon. by appointment.

Following their dream, two couples, the Klindts and the Heins, started a microwinery in 1989. Naming it was easy, since both women partners bear the name Claudia. The winery produces 1200 cases a year of Chardonnay, Pinot Noir and Zinfandel. They now purchase Mendocino grapes, but future plans include a vineyard. When weather permits, tasting is on the deck, which offers a view.

CLINE CELLARS

6 miles south of Sonoma at 24737 Arnold Dr., 95476. (707) 935-4310; FAX (707) 935-4319. Open for tasting daily 10 a.m. to 6 p.m.; tours by appointment. Closed Dec. 25. $1 tasting fee for reserve or library wines.

The emphasis at Cline Cellars is on Rhône varietals and Zinfandel. Founded in 1982, the winery moved to the Carneros district of Sonoma County in 1991, but most of the grapes still come from the family vineyards in Oakley where Cline's reputation was established; the sandy, phylloxera-resistant soil supports vines from 40 to 100 years old. Brothers Fred and Matt Cline vinify and blend Mourvedre, Carignane, Syrah, Sémillon and Alicante bouschet for about 25,000 cases each year. There are ponds populated by koi, turtles and frogs, eucalyptus-shaded picnic tables and more than 200 varieties of roses that provide a picturesque setting for the restored 1854 farmhouse housing the tasting room.

CLOS DU BOIS

19410 Geyserville Ave., Geyserville (mailing address: P.O. Box 940, 95441). (707) 857-3100, (800) 222-3189; FAX (707) 857-3229. Open for tasting daily 10 a.m. to 4:30 p.m. Closed Jan. 1, Easter, Thanksgiving, Dec. 25 and for special events.

Clos du Bois began with 2000 cases in 1974, and has grown to be the largest producer of fine wines in Sonoma County: Sauvignon Blanc, Gewürztraminer, Pinot Noir, Merlot, Cabernet Sauvignon, Zinfandel and four vine-designated wines. They are also the largest producer of barrel-fermented Chardonnays in America. For seven consecutive years *Wine & Spirits* magazine has given Clos du Bois top honors as "winery of the year."

CLOS DU VAL WINE COMPANY, LTD.

5 miles north of Napa at 5330 Silverado Tr. (mailing address: P.O. Box 4350, 94558). (707) 259-2200. Open for tasting daily 10 a.m. to 5 p.m.; tours by appointment. $3 tasting fee.

Launched in 1972, Clos du Val combines winemaker Bernard Portet's French enological background with American technology. The winery produces Merlot, Zinfandel, Cabernet Sauvignon and Sémillon varietal wines from estate vineyards adjacent to the early California-style winery. Pinot Noir and Chardonnay are produced from their vineyards in the Carneros district.

CLOS PEGASE

1 mile south of Calistoga at 1060 Dunaweal Ln. (mailing address: P.O. Box 305, 94515). (707) 942-4981; FAX (707) 942-4993. Open for tasting daily 10:30 a.m. to 5 p.m.; tours daily at 11 a.m. and 2 p.m. $2.50 tasting fee.

Myth and art pervade Jan Shrem's winery. Sculptures, paintings and reliefs adorn every wall and corner of the tasting room and the storage and production areas. Shrem planned a contest, which was sponsored by the San Francisco Museum of Modern Art, for

Michelle De Lude

The vivid contrast of avant-garde architecture and antique winemaking equipment provides a lively experience for visitors to the Codorniu Napa Winery.

the design of his winery. The contest winner, Princeton architect Michael Graves, created a Greco-Roman stucco edifice that is very dramatic. Wine writer James Halliday described it as "part winery, part museum and part Parthenon...." The winery stores 5000 barrels in caves measuring 22,000 square feet and holding a constant temperature of 60 degrees Fahrenheit and humidity at 90 percent. The winery produces Cabernet Sauvignon, Chardonnay and Merlot from more than 400 acres of vineyards in Calistoga, St. Helena and Carneros. Slide shows scheduled for the third Saturday of each month fill up quickly; reservations are suggested.

CODORNIU NAPA
3½ miles west of SR 29, off SR 12/121 via Dealy Ln. at 1345 Henry Rd., Napa 94559. (707) 224-1668; FAX (707) 224-1672. Open for tasting and tours daily; Mon. through Thur. 10 a.m. to 5 p.m., Fri. through Sun. to 3 p.m. $4 tasting fee.

The Codorniu family made Spain's first *méthode champenoise* sparkling wine in 1872, and in 1991 they opened their first sparkling wine facility outside Spain in the Carneros district of Napa County. The earth-covered building, designed by Domingo Triay, is covered with grasses indigenous to California. A striking prism window, fountains, falls and pools adorn the entrance to the winery. Inside, exhibits of changing and permanent art work and antique wine-making equipment can be seen.

CONN CREEK WINERY
South of Rutherford Cross Rd. at 8711 Silverado Tr., St. Helena 94574. (707) 963-5133. Open for tasting daily 10 a.m. to 4 p.m.; tours by appointment.

Conn Creek spent its first five years in a leased, century-old stone building north of St. Helena. In 1979 a new, energy-efficient winery was built on the Silverado Trail. Production focuses on Cabernet Sauvignon, Merlot and a Meritage blend from grapes grown in vineyards at Yountville and near St. Helena.

COSENTINO WINERY
South of Yount Hill Rd. at 7415 St. Helena Hwy., Yountville (mailing address: SR 29, P.O. Box 2818, 94599). (707) 944-1220. Open for tasting daily 10 a.m. to 5 p.m. $2 tasting fee includes souvenir glass, refundable with purchase.

Mitch Cosentino crushed his first wine in 1980. In 1985 he designed and established his winery in the Napa Valley. Cosentino produces Meritage (red and white wines from the traditional Bordeaux-grape varieties) as well as Cabernet Sauvignon, Cabernet Franc, Chardonnay, Merlot, Pinot Noir, Zinfandel, Nebbiolo and Sangiovese. Port and dessert wine are produced in limited quantities. Total winery production is 18,000 cases annually.

CUVAISON
4550 Silverado Tr., Calistoga 94515. (707) 942-6266. Open for tasting daily 10 a.m. to 5 p.m.; tours by appointment only. Tasting fee includes complimentary glass.

Cuvaison, whose name is the French word for "wine fermenting on the skins," was established in 1969. The winery makes Chardonnay, Reserve Chardonnay, Pinot Noir, Cabernet Sauvignon and Merlot from grapes grown in their Carneros Estate Vineyard; it also produces Cabernet Sauvignon from grapes in the heart of Napa Valley. Visitors to the facility may use the oak-shaded picnic facilities and visit the unique tasting room and gift shop.

DAVIS BYNUM WINERY
8 miles west of Healdsburg at 8075 Westside Rd., 95448. (707) 433-5852. Open for tasting daily 10 a.m. to 5 p.m.; tours by appointment only.

Bottling lines can take up hundreds of square feet, or they can fit into the back of a small truck, like this one at Dehlinger.

Michelle De Lude

Davis Bynum has been in the Russian River Valley for 30 years. In 1973, he was the first to produce Pinot Noir exclusively from grapes in this area. Production now includes a full range of varietals. There are beautifully land-scaped picnic grounds for visitors.

DEER PARK WINERY

5 miles northeast of St. Helena at junction of Sanitarium and Deer Park rds.; 1000 Deer Park Rd., Deer Park 94576. (707) 963-5411. Open for tasting and guided tours by appointment only, Fri. and Sat. 10 a.m. to 5 p.m.; mid-Apr. through Nov. also open Sun. 1 to 5 p.m.

Deer Park Winery occupies the origin-al site of Sutter Home Winery, on a hillside in the foothills of Howell Mountain. The two-story stone winery was constructed in 1891. Surviving Prohibition, it changed hands several times. In 1979, operations resumed under the current owners, the Knapps and the Clarks. This small, family owned winery produces 3000 cases of Zinfandel and Petite Sirah every year.

DEHLINGER WINERY

6300 Guerneville Rd., Sebastopol 95472. (707) 823-2378. Open for tasting and tours Fri. through Mon. 10 a.m. to 5 p.m.

Tom Dehlinger planted 14 acres of premium grape vines in 1975 on his ranch north of Sebastopol. He now pro-duces about 8000 cases per year of Chardonnay, Pinot Noir, Merlot and Syrah exclusively from his 50-acre vine-yard in the Russian River Valley. Dehlinger uses traditional winemaking practices aimed at the production of aromatic and flavorful table wines.

DELOACH VINEYARDS

5 miles west of Santa Rosa at 1791 Olivet Rd., 95401. (707) 526-9111. Open for tasting daily 10 a.m. to 4:30 p.m.; tours Mon. through Fri. at 2 p.m., and Sat. and Sun. at 11 a.m. and 2 p.m.

DeLoach Vineyards' redwood winery stands in the midst of vineyards, some dating to 1905. The DeLoach family now produces 130,000 cases annually of a large number of premium varietal wines from more than 350 acres of grapes grown in the Russian River Valley. Picnic facilities and horseshoe pits under the redwood trees are adjacent to the winery, and the tasting room displays work by local artists.

DELORIMIER WINERY

Off US 101 to 2001 SR 128, Geyserville 95441. (707) 857-2000. Open for tasting and self-guided tours Thur. through Mon. 10 a.m. to 4:30 p.m.; guided tours of the winery and vineyard by appointment.

Al and Sandy deLorimier use a variety of innovative techniques on their 65-acre vineyard to produce 5000 cases of Red and White Meritage, Chardonnay and Late Harvest wine. Al deLorimier is a renowned pediatric surgeon; his wife, Sandy deLorimier, is in charge of the winery's image and label design.

DE MOOR WINERY

2 miles north of Yountville at 7481 SR 29 (mailing address: P.O. Box 348, Oakville 94562). (707) 944-2565; FAX (707) 944-0250. Open for tasting daily, Jun. through Aug. 10:30 a.m. to 5:30 p.m.; Sept. through May 10 a.m. to 5 p.m. $2 tasting fee includes souvenir glass.

De Moor's unique geodesic-domed visitors's center and winery are a Napa Valley landmark. It was built in 1973 and vineyards were planted surrounding the site. Originally called Napa Cellars, it then became De Moor, and state-of-the-art equipment was installed at the facility. Case production is now 25,000 annually of five varietals: Cabernet Sauvignon, Zinfandel, Chardonnay, Chenin Blanc and Sauvignon Blanc. Picnic facilities are available.

Domaine Carneros takes its name from the Carneros region, known for its Chardonnay and Pinot Noir grapes.

Michelle De Lude

DOMAINE CARNEROS

5½ miles southwest of Napa off SR 12/121 at 1240 Duhig Rd. (mailing address: P.O. Box 5420, 94581). (707) 257-0101; FAX (707) 257-3020. Open for tasting, retail sales and tours daily 10:30 a.m. to 6 p.m.; tours Sat. and Sun. on the hour from 11 a.m. to 3 p.m.; tours Mon. through Fri. at 11 a.m., 1 and 3 p.m. $4 tasting fee per glass includes hors d'oeuvres.

Hand-picking grapes in Dry Creek Valley.

Dry Creek Vineyard

Established in the Carneros region in 1987, Domaine Carneros is already considered a regional landmark. This spectacular *méthode champenoise* sparkling wine facility was inspired by the Chateau de la Marquetterie, the historic 18th-century Champagne residence owned by the principle founder of Domaine Carneros, Champagne Taittinger of Reims, France. Production now stands at 45,000 cases per year, using grapes grown only in the Carneros region.

DOMAINE CHANDON

West of SR 29 off California Dr. in Yountville (mailing address: P.O. Box 2470, 94599). (707) 944-2280 (winery); (800) 736-2892 (restaurant reservations). Open for tasting and tours May through Oct., daily 11 a.m. to 6 p.m.; Nov. through Apr., Wed. through Sun. 11 a.m. to 6 p.m. Tours on the hour 11 a.m. to 5 p.m. $3 to $5 tasting fee per glass.

Domaine Chandon is a subsidiary of Moët-Hennessy Louis Vuitton of France, a prestigious producer of luxury items. Established in 1973, the winery now makes five styles of California sparkling wine by the traditional *méthode champ-*

enoise. On a 45-minute tour, visitors to the winery learn about all phases of this process, from tirage and aging to riddling and disgorging. Adjacent to the tasting salon is the winery's restaurant, which serves lunch and dinner.

DOMAINE ST. GEORGE WINERY & VINEYARDS

2 miles southeast of Healdsburg off Old Redwood Hwy. at 1141 Grant Ave. (mailing address: P.O. Box 548, 95448). (707) 433-5508. Open for retail sales Mon. through Fri. 10 a.m. to 4 p.m. No tasting; tours by appointment only. Closed holidays.

The former jug-wine oriented Cambiaso winery has modernized and expanded, resulting in a shift in emphasis toward vintage-dated varietals. Visitors to the hillside winery today will see a modern facility located directly adjacent to the old, rustic cellar.

DRY CREEK VINEYARD

4 miles northwest of Healdsburg at Dry Creek and Lambert Bridge rds. (mailing address: P.O. Box T, 95448). (707) 433-1000. Open for tasting daily 10:30 a.m. to 4:30 p.m.

Dry Creek Vineyard

Dry Creek Vineyard was the first winery built in Sonoma County after Prohibition ended.

Dry Creek was Sonoma County's first new winery to be built in Dry Creek Valley since Prohibition. Founded in 1972 by David Stare, the winery's 1000 awards for excellence reflect quality and consistency in this family owned operation. Producing about 100,000 cases of premium wines per year, Dry Creek Vineyard is best known for its Fumé Blanc, Zinfandel, Cabernet Sauvignon and Chardonnay. There are picnic facilities for visitors.

DUNNEWOOD VINEYARDS & WINERY

2399 N. State St., Ukiah 95470. (707) 462-2987; FAX (707) 462-0323. Open for tasting daily 10 a.m. to 5 p.m.; one-hour tours by appointment.

Dunnewood Vineyards occupies the facilities of the former Cresta Blanca Winery, which was founded in the 1880s by Charles Wetmore. The Cresta Blanca brand and the winery were purchased by Guild Wineries and Distilleries (makers of Cook's sparkling wine) in the late 1960s, and Guild in turn was bought by Canandaigua Wine Company, the second largest wine company in the nation. Fruit for the annual 120,000 cases of wine comes from vineyards in Mendocino, Napa and Sonoma counties, with production expected to increase to 250,000 cases by 1995. Chardonnay comprises about half of the winery's releases, with lesser amounts of Merlot and Cabernet Sauvignon, Gamay Beaujolais, Pinot Noir, Sauvignon Blanc and White Zinfandel. A gift and gourmet shop, picnic deli items, and a patio with picnic tables under the apple trees are available for visitors.

ELIZABETH VINEYARDS

6 miles north of Ukiah, 2 miles off US 101 at 8591 Colony Dr., Redwood Valley 95470. (707) 463-2662. Open for tasting and vineyard tours by appointment only.

Established in 1987 in the beautiful Redwood Valley, this 50-acre winery produces 800 cases of Chardonnay and Zinfandel, both wines Orange County Gold Medal winners. The grapes are grown on hillside and rolling benchland vineyards cooled by Pacific Ocean breezes. There are picnic facilities for visitors.

FERRARI-CARANO VINEYARDS AND WINERY

10 miles north of Healdsburg at 8761 Dry Creek Rd., 95448. (707) 996-1238. Open for tasting daily 10 a.m. to 5 p.m.; tours by appointment.

At the north end of the picturesque Dry Creek Valley, just south of Lake Sonoma, is family owned Ferrari-Carano Vineyards and Winery. Founded in 1981 by Don and Rhonda Carano, Ferrari-Carano wines are created from hillside and valley vineyards spread over 50 miles. Flower gardens surround the Italian villa-style hospitality center, Villa Fiore, which houses the winery and tasting room. Samples of Chardonnay, Chardonnay Reserve, Merlot, Cabernet Sauvignon, Zinfandel and Eldorado Gold late harvest dessert wine are offered; also available are library vintages and limited production wines.

FETZER VINEYARDS

At the Valley Oaks Food and Wine Center in Hopland, 1 mile east at junction of US 101 and SR 175; 13601 East Side Rd. (mailing address: P.O. Box 611, 95449). (707) 744-1250 (winery and garden hospitality), 744-1737 (tasting room); FAX (707) 744-1250. Open for tasting daily 10 a.m. to 5 p.m.; garden tours from Jun. through Aug. at 11 a.m. and 3 p.m. (call to confirm).

The Valley Oaks Ranch was founded in 1844 when Fernando Feliz built his adobe house on the property. Originally part of a Mexican land grant, the ranch has had only five owners in its history.

The Fetzer family purchased it in 1984 and developed the Fetzer Food and Wine Center at Valley Oaks, featuring gourmet deli foods, gifts, clothing and an art gallery. In 1992 Brown-Forman, based in Louisville, Kentucky, purchased the Fetzer and Bel Arbors brand names, as well as the Hopland Winery and the Fetzer Food and Wine Center. There are also a play and picnic area and a bed and breakfast inn at Valley Oaks.

FIELD STONE WINERY

9 miles east of Healdsburg at 10075 SR 128, 95448. (707) 433-7266; FAX (707) 433-2231. Open for tasting daily 10 a.m. to 5 p.m.; comprehensive tours by appointment only. Closed Easter, Thanksgiving and Dec. 25.

Fronted by a handsome stone wall, this small winery is tucked underground in an Alexander Valley hillside. Annual production is 10,000 cases. Current offerings include five varietal wines: Sauvignon Blanc, Chardonnay, Gewürztraminer, Cabernet Sauvignon and Petite Sirah. A gift shop, refrigerated deli items, and a picnic area under spreading oaks are available for guests.

FISHER VINEYARDS

6200 St. Helena Rd., Santa Rosa, 95404. (707) 539-7511. No tasting; tours and sales by appointment.

Located at an elevation of 1200 feet on the western slope of the Mayacamas Mountains, Fred Fisher's vineyards include plantings of Chardonnay and Cabernet Sauvignon dating from 1974. The small family winery was constructed of redwood and Douglas fir grown on the property.

FLORA SPRINGS WINE COMPANY

1½ miles south of St. Helena at 1978 W. Zinfandel Ln., 94574. (707) 963-5711. Open for tasting and tours by appointment Mon. through Sat.; a one-hour vineyard tour, available on request, is of special interest during the fall harvest.

The fieldstone winery structure at Flora Springs was built during the late 19th century. After Prohibition it served for a time as a cellar for Louis M. Martini's wines, and in 1977 the Komes and Garvey families bought the property. Some 400 acres produce about 2000 tons of grapes each year, with about 30 percent of the crop selected for Flora Springs premium wines. The winery specializes in Cabernet Sauvignon, Chardonnay, Merlot, Sauvignon Blanc and a proprietary Bordeaux-style claret, for an annual output of about 40,000 cases per year.

FOLIE A DEUX WINERY
2 miles north of St. Helena at 3070 SR 29, 94574. (800) 473-4454. Open for tasting and tours daily 11 a.m. to 5 p.m.

In 1981 two psychiatrists gave in to their delusions and opened this small winery, hence the name "Folie a deux"—a psychiatric term meaning "a shared fantasy or delusion." The winery produces 15,000 cases per year of Chardonnay, dry Chenin Blanc, Cabernet Sauvignon, and a *méthode champenoise* Napa Valley Sparkling Wine, Fantasie. Perched on a knoll overlooking the estate's 22-acre vineyard is an old farmhouse now housing the winery. Visitors are welcome to picnic.

FOPPIANO VINEYARDS
2 miles south of Healdsburg at 12707 Old Redwood Hwy. (mailing address: P.O. Box 606, 95448). (707) 433-7272; FAX (707) 433-0565. Open for tasting and self-guided vineyard tours daily 10 a.m. to 4:30 p.m.; guided winery tours by appointment only.

Giovanni "John" Foppiano purchased his land in the Russian River Valley in 1896, although parts of the winery date as far back as 1880. Although fermentation and aging are done primarily in

stainless steel tanks and small oak cooperage, a few rare redwood storage tanks that date prior to Prohibition are still used for the red wines. The winery is known for its Petite Sirah, but also makes five varietal and two blended wines.

FRANCISCAN ESTATES
1 mile north of Rutherford at junction SR 29 and Galleron Rd. (mailing address: P.O. Box 407, 94573). (707) 963-7111; FAX (707) 963-7867. Open for tasting daily 10 a.m. to 5 p.m. Closed Jan. 1, Easter, Thanksgiving and Dec. 25. $2 tasting fee includes souvenir glass.

Franciscan is part of an estate group that produces premium varietal wine from select regions of Napa, Sonoma and Monterey counties in California, and from Chile. There is a whimsical *Rutherford Bench* sculpture in front of the winery that visitors may use for photo opportunities. The tasting room features Franciscan Vineyards, Estancia and Mount Veeder wines; Mount Veeder vertical tastings are conducted on Saturday and Sunday.

FREEMARK ABBEY WINERY
2 miles north of St. Helena on SR 29 (mailing address: P.O. Box 410, 94574). (707) 963-9694. Open for tasting and tours. May 1 through Sep. 30, daily from 10 a.m. to 5 p.m.; tours at 2 p.m. Rest of year call for days and hours of operation. Tasting fee includes logo glass.

The stone building occupied by the winery dates to 1895, but Freemark Abbey itself was established in 1967, when new owners acquired the property and began a program of modernization and expansion. Now producing 38,000 cases a year, Freemark Abbey concentrates on four varietal wines: Cabernet Sauvignon, Chardonnay, Merlot and Riesling. The tasting room fireplace is lit in winter; in spring and summer visitors may sit in the garden terrace.

FREY VINEYARDS
14000 Tomki Rd., Redwood Valley 95470. (707) 485-5177. Open for tasting and tours daily by appointment only.

The Frey family operates California's first and largest organic winery on their ranch near the head of the Russian River in Redwood Valley. The vineyards are dry-farmed without insecticides or herbicides, and the three white and three red wines are made without chemical additives.

FROG'S LEAP WINERY
8815 Conn Creek Rd., Rutherford (mailing address: P.O. Box 189, 94573). (707) 963-4704. Open for tasting and tours Mon. through Fri. by appointment.

Frog's Leap was founded in 1981 at a spot along the Mill Creek known as the Frog Farm. An old ledger revealed that around the turn of the 20th century, frogs were raised there and sold for 33 cents a dozen—they were probably destined for the tables of Victorian San Francisco gourmets. In 1994, John and Julie Williams moved the winery production facility and offices to the historic Red Barn property in Rutherford. Originally built in 1884 as the Adamson Winery, the Red Barn Ranch has been restored and saw its first harvest in 98 years. Frog's Leap growers are committed to sustainable, organic agriculture and their goal is to have fun making elegant wines with superb balance. Sauvignon Blanc, Zinfandel, Cabernet Sauvignon, Carneros Chardonnay and Merlot wines are produced by Frog's Leap.

GABRIELLI WINERY
10 miles north of Ukiah on US 101 at 10950 West Rd., Redwood Valley 95470. (707) 485-1221. Open for informal tours daily 10 a.m. to 5 p.m.; large groups should call ahead to reserve.

Gabrielli is a small, family oriented farm and winery founded in 1989 and dedicated to producing intense, fine

Mendocino wines. Its annual production of 8000 cases includes Chardonnay, Ascenza, Zinfandel, Riesling and Pinot Noir. Picnic facilities are available for visitors.

GERMAIN-ROBIN/ALAMBIC
At south end of Ukiah, junction of SR 253 and US 101; 3001 S. State St. (mailing address: P.O. Box 175, 95482). (707) 462-0314. Warehouse location open for sales daily 8 a.m. to 4 p.m.; guided tours of the distillery are by appointment only; call (707) 462-3221 for directions.

The company was founded by Hubert Germain-Robin, who brought an antique cognac still to Mendocino County. Hubert, whose family has produced cognac since 1782, uses traditional methods which have been almost abandoned in France. Each year he hand-distills 80 barrels of a true connoisseur's brandy, cellared in Limousin oak. A custom blend is sold to the White House, where Germain-Robin was served at the 1987 Reagan-Gorbachev summit, the 1992 Bush celebration and the 1993 Clinton Inaugural.

GEYSER PEAK WINERY
1 mile north of Geyserville off US 101 at 22281 Chianti Rd., 95441. (707) 857-9400, (800) 255-9463. Open for tasting daily 10 a.m. to 5 p.m.; tours by appointment only. Closed major holidays.

Geyser Peak Winery was founded in 1880 by winemaker Augustus Quitzow, who constructed the winery two years later on a hillside opposite Geyser Peak Mountain. The impressive ivy-covered buildings have stained glass windows and are graced by a fountain at the entrance. A picnic area is located beside the winery. Now owned by the Trione family, the winery produces a large number of varietal wines and a red Meritage blend under the direction of winemaker Daryl Groom. Groom was the first winemaker to produce the traditional Australian blend of Sémillon and

Chardonnay in the United States. Refrigerated deli items are sold in the tasting room and there is a gift shop.

GIRARD WINERY

2 miles east of Oakville at 7717 Silverado Tr. (mailing address: P.O. Box 105, 94562). (707) 944-8577. Open for tasting and tours daily 11 a.m. to 4:30 p.m.

The 45-acre vineyard surrounding the Girard winery was planted to Cabernet Sauvignon and Chardonnay in 1968. The Girard family built their modern winery in 1980 and crushed their first vintage that fall. The winery also produces Chenin Blanc and Zinfandel.

GLORIA FERRER CHAMPAGNE CAVES

5 miles south of Sonoma at 23555 Carneros Hwy. (mailing address: P.O. Box 1427, 95476). (707) 996-7256. Open for tasting daily 10:30 a.m. to 5:30 p.m.; tours hourly 11 a.m. to 4 p.m. Tasting fee $3 to $5.

The Ferrer family is the world's largest producer of *méthode champenoise* sparkling wines, the best known of which is Freixenet, vinified in Cataluna in northeastern Spain. In 1986, in the Carneros region south of Sonoma, their large, Catalan-Romanesque-style winery was built on a hill overlooking acres of recently planted vineyards. On informative tours, visitors can see the underground aging caves and other production facilities.

GREENWOOD RIDGE VINEYARDS

Tasting room located 3 miles north of Philo at 5501 SR 128, 95466. (707) 895-2002. Open for tasting daily; Jun. through Aug. 10 a.m. to 6 p.m.; Sept. through May 10 a.m. to 5 p.m. Tours of winery by appointment. Closed Jan. 1, Thanksgiving, and Dec. 25.

This small winery opened in 1980 on a 1400-foot-high ridge adjacent to the Anderson Valley. The eight-acre vineyard was planted in 1972 to Riesling, Merlot and Cabernet Sauvignon. Some of the fruit contributes to its 6000-case annual output. Each July, the winery hosts the light-hearted California Wine Tasting Championships; see Annual Events.

GRGICH HILLS CELLAR

1829 St. Helena Hwy., Rutherford (mailing address: P.O. Box 450, 94573). (707) 963-2784. Open for tasting daily 9:30 a.m. to 4:30 p.m.; tours by appointment.

Miljenko "Mike" Grgich has been making wine in the Napa Valley since 1958; in 1977 he and his partner, Austin Hills, built the winery. Production is about 60,000 cases per year of Sauvignon Blanc, Cabernet Sauvignon and Zinfandel, with an emphasis on Chardonnay.

GROTH VINEYARDS & WINERY

2 miles east of SR 29 at 750 Oakville Crossroad, Oakville 94562. (707) 944-0290. Open Tue. through Sat. 10 a.m. to 4 p.m. by appointment.

The Groth family purchased 164 acres of Napa Valley vineyards in 1981-82 and, using their own grapes, immediately set about making Chardonnay, Sauvignon Blanc, Merlot and Cabernet Sauvignon. Winemaker Michael Weis now produces about 40,000 cases annually of the three varietals. The new, three-level winery in the Oakville area was completed in 1990.

GUNDLACH-BUNDSCHU WINERY

2 miles east of Sonoma via Napa St. and 8th St. E. at 2000 Denmark St., Vineburg 95487. (707) 938-5277. Open for tasting daily 11 a.m. to 4:30 p.m.; tours by appointment. Closed major holidays.

The partnership formed by Jacob Gundlach and Charles Bundschu in

1862 has survived for five generations. The 1906 San Francisco earthquake destroyed the winery's entire inventory, and finally, Prohibition ended their production. The Bundschu family remained growers until reentering the winemaking business in the late 1960s, and today they make 50,000 cases per year of varietal and blended wines. They are the only American producers of Kleinberger (available only at the winery). Tasting is in the ivy-covered, 134-year-old winery building, which overlooks a small pond. Stone frogs, rabbits and dwarves impart a sense of whimsy to the landscape, and a short, strenuous hike leads to a beautiful view of Sonoma Valley. The last half-mile of the road to the winery is one-lane wide with turnouts.

HAKUSAN SAKE GARDENS

South of Napa on SR 29 at SR 12, exit Kelly Rd. to 1 Executive Wy., 94558. (707) 258-6160, (800) HAKUSAN. Open for tasting and self-guided tours daily 9 a.m. to 6 p.m. Closed Jan. 1, Easter, Thanksgiving, and Dec. 25.

Situated on 20 acres and surrounded by beautiful Japanese gardens, the Kohnan Inc. facility is the realization of founder Toyokichi Hombo's dream. Built in 1989, this state-of-the-art sakery can produce up to 250,000 cases using rice grown in the Sacramento Valley. Production includes dry sake (rice wine), two dessert sakes and one cooking sake. A gift shop and art gallery are on the premises.

HANDLEY CELLARS

6 miles northwest of Philo at 3151 SR 128 (mailing address: P.O. Box 66, 95466). (707) 895-3876, 895-2190. Open for tasting daily; Nov. to Feb. 11 a.m. to 5 p.m., and Jun. through Aug. to 6 p.m.; tours by appointment.

Handley began in 1982 as a small family winery in the basement of the owner's home. Now more than 15,000 cases a

year of Chardonnay, Gewürztraminer, Pinot Noir, Sauvignon Blanc and *méthode champenoise* sparkling wine are produced from grapes grown in the Anderson and Dry Creek valleys. A modern wood-sided winery and tasting room was completed in 1987. Picnicking facilities are available, and the owner's collection of folk art may be viewed in the tasting room.

HEITZ WINE CELLARS

2½ miles south of St. Helena at 436 St. Helena Hwy. S., 94574. (707) 963-3542. Open for tasting daily 11 a.m. to 4:30 p.m. Tours by appointment Mon. through Fri. Closed major holidays.

Established in 1961 by Joe and Alice Heitz, today the business is a family operation with children David, Kathleen and Rollie. They are dedicated to producing outstanding Cabernet Sauvignon and Chardonnay.

THE HESS COLLECTION WINERY

4411 Redwood Rd., Napa (mailing address: P.O. Box 4140, 94558). (707) 255-1144; FAX (707) 253-1682. Open for tasting and self-guided tours daily 10 a.m. to 4 p.m. Closed Jan. 1, Easter, Thanksgiving and Dec. 25. $2.50 tasting fee.

Swiss entrepreneur Donald Hess chose the steep sides of Mount Veeder for his venture into California winemaking. Bronze plaques and a brochure guide visitors to views overlooking winery operations and two upper floors of art galleries (accessible by stair and elevator). A 12-minute audiovisual presentation screens every half hour and shows the seasonal challenges unique to mountain vineyards. Of the property's 900 acres, 285 are planted to Chardonnay and Cabernet Sauvignon (the winery's two varietals), and small amounts of red Bordeaux grapes are grown for blending purposes. Visitors may purchase a catalog of the contemporary art work on display.

Hopland was named for the hops grown so successfully in Mendocino and northern Sonoma counties. Built in 1905, these restored buildings have provided a name and a home for the Hop Kiln Winery since 1975.

HIDDEN CELLARS
2 miles west of Talmage off US 101 at 1500 Ruddick-Cunningham Rd. (mailing address: P.O. Box 448, Ukiah, 95481). (707) 462-0301. Tasting and tours by appointment only.

Dennis Patton was a local farmer and home winemaker when he founded Hidden Cellars in 1981. He started the first winery on Mill Creek with a hand-operated basket press and a few used dairy tanks. In 1983, he moved the operations to Hildreth Ranch, where he produces Chardonnay, Zinfandel, Sauvignon Blanc and Johannisberg Riesling. All wines are made from Mendocino County grapes, and production is now 25,000 cases per year. Visitors are welcome to picnic in the tree-shaded picnic area.

THE HOP KILN WINERY
6 miles southwest of Healdsburg at 6050 Westside Rd., 95448. (707) 433-6491. Open for tasting daily 10 a.m. to 5 p.m.

This historic structure has been a local landmark since 1905, when it was built as a hops drying barn. In 1975 the restored kilns became a bonded winery, which now yields 10,000 cases of wine yearly. Seven varietal wines are produced in limited quantities with a special emphasis on Zinfandel. The historic tasting room overlooks the Russian River Valley, and visitors can view the collection of local artwork. The picnic area is beside a large pond.

HUSCH VINEYARDS
5 miles northwest of Philo at 4400 SR 128, 95466. (707) 895-3216. Open for tasting and self-guided vineyard tours daily; Jun. through Aug. 10 a.m. to 6 p.m., rest of year to 5 p.m. Winery tours by appointment only.

The winery began in 1971 on a 23-acre plot in the cool Anderson Valley. Anthony Husch and his family crushed their grapes on the patio of their home until the winery building was built in 1974. Now owned by the Oswald family, the small winery produces its varietal wines from estate-grown Gewürztraminer, Chardonnay, Sauvignon Blanc, Chenin Blanc, Cabernet Sauvignon and Pinot Noir grapes. A brochure available in the tasting room directs visitors on a tour of the vineyard. Picnic tables are set under grape arbors.

IRON HORSE VINEYARDS
9786 Ross Station Rd., Sebastopol 95472. (707) 887-1507. Tasting by appointment only, Sat. 9 a.m. to 3:30 p.m. Tours with tasting are by appointment Mon. through Fri. at 10 a.m. and 2 p.m.

Founded in 1979, Iron Horse presently produces Cabernet Sauvignon, Chardonnay, Pinot Noir and Sauvignon Blanc table wine and several different sparkling wines. Grapes are grown in the 140-acre home vineyard in the western foothills of Sonoma County and at the winemaker's vineyard in the Alexander Valley. The current production level is 38,000 cases per year.

J. FRITZ WINERY
3 miles south of Cloverdale at 24691 Dutcher Creek Rd., 95425. (707) 894-3389. Open for tasting daily 10:30 a.m. to 4:30 p.m. Tours by appointment.

Since 1979, Jay and Barbara Fritz's subterranean winery has produced award-winning Sauvignon Blanc, Chardonnay and Zinfandel. Visitors are welcome to picnic on the grounds with views overlooking the vineyards.

J. PEDRONCELLI WINERY
1 mile west of Geyserville at 1220 Canyon Rd., 95441. (707) 857-3531, (800) 836-3894. Open for tasting daily 10 a.m. to 5 p.m. Tours by appointment.

Wholesale grocer John Canata built the winery and planted 90 acres of adjoining vineyards in 1904. In 1927, John Pedroncelli Sr. bought the property, which reminded him of his native Italy. When Prohibition ended, the winery sold bulk wine for a time before

releasing wine with the Pedroncelli name on the label; in 1949, Zinfandel became the winery's first varietally labeled release. Now owned by John Jr. and Jim Pedroncelli, the winery makes a number of varietals with as little handling as possible during the winemaking process; most wines are made completely from the stated variety. Rotating art exhibits change every six weeks; a picnic area and boccie court are available to visitors.

JEPSON VINEYARDS, WINERY & DISTILLERY
3 miles north of Hopland at 10400 S. US 101, Ukiah 95482. (707) 468-8936; FAX (707) 468-0362. Open for tasting daily 10 a.m. to 5 p.m. Tours by appointment only.

Nestled in the rolling hills of Mendocino County is one of California's most picturesque wineries. The vineyards run alongside the Russian River and a 100-year-old farmhouse now serves as an office. Jepson's specialties are estate-grown and bottled Chardonnay, Champagne and Brandy. Champagne is made from Chardonnay grapes, part of which have been barrel-fermented, resulting in a dry, delicate taste. Also produced is a *méthode champenoise* champagne. Jepson Rare Brandy is aged five years in small oak barrels and estate-bottled in an authentic alembic pot still from France. There are picnic facilities and a gift shop for visitors.

JOHNSON'S ALEXANDER VALLEY WINES
7 miles southeast of Geyserville at 8333 SR 128, Healdsburg 95448. (707) 433-2319. Open for tasting and tours daily 10 a.m. to 5 p.m.

The Johnsons started farming in the Alexander Valley in 1952, but their first premium grapes weren't planted until 1966. A decade later the winery was completed. Visitors are invited to picnic and listen to the 1924 theater pipe organ.

JOSEPH PHELPS VINEYARDS

2 miles southeast of St. Helena off Silverado Tr. at 200 Taplin Rd. (mailing address: P.O. Box 1031, 94574). (707) 963-2745. Open for tasting and tours by appointment, daily 9 a.m. to 4 p.m.

Built in 1973, Joseph Phelps Vineyards is a tribute to the arts of architecture and winemaking. Situated on a hillside, the redwood winery is designed to blend with the rolling hills and vineyards that surround it. There is a spectacular view of the Napa Valley with its native California oaks, a picturesque pond and meticulously tended vineyards. Phelps produces 100,000 cases annually of respected red and white varietals, including Insignia, Cabernet Sauvignon, Chardonnay, Merlot, Sauvignon Blanc, Syrah, Viognier and several dessert wines.

KENDALL JACKSON WINE COUNTRY STORE

North of Healdsburg on US 101, exit Central Healdsburg to 337 Healdsburg Ave., 95448. (707) 433-7102; FAX (707) 433-6215. Open for tasting daily 10 a.m. to 4:30 p.m.

This enterprise began as one family's escape from city life, and now "K-J", as the winery is popularly known, is a success story. Jess Jackson identified and met the need for a desirable, high quality varietal wine at an acceptable price. In 19 short years, Kendall Jackson's annual production has grown to 1.2 million cases of premium and super-premium wines, distributed nationally. In addition, Jackson farms about 4000 acres of vineyards and has also integrated barrel production in France.

KENWOOD VINEYARDS

9592 Sonoma Hwy., Kenwood (mailing address: P.O. Box 447, 95452). (707)

833-5891. Open for tasting daily 10 a.m. to 4:30 p.m.; tours by appointment.

Established in 1906, the old Pagani Brothers winery was acquired by the Lee family in 1970. Since then, it has undergone a process of steady growth and modernization. Today the winery emphasizes the production of premium white and red varietal wines, including Sauvignon Blanc, Cabernet Sauvignon, Zinfandel and Merlot.

KONOCTI WINERY

At junction of SR 29 and Thomas Dr., Kelseyville (mailing address: P.O. Box 890, 95451). (707) 279-4395. Open for tasting Mon. through Sat. 10 a.m. to 5 p.m., Sun. 11 a.m. to 5 p.m.; tours by appointment.

Konocti is a cooperative winery founded by an association of Lake County growers and named after Mt. Konocti, the area's 4200-foot inactive volcano. Grapes from 400 acres of vineyards are made into varietal wines in a functional, insulated metal building which sits in the midst of an experimental vineyard. The first crush occurred in 1974; now the capacity stands at 50,000 cases per year. Visitors are invited to use the picnic area and visit the gift shop.

KONRAD ESTATE WINERY

8 miles north of Ukiah off US 101 at 3620 Rd. B, Redwood Valley 95470. (707) 485-0323. Open for tasting and tours daily; Mar. through Nov. 10 a.m. to 5 p.m., Dec. through Feb. to 4 p.m.

Konrad Estate Winery is located near the north end of California's coastal growing region, on an 1100-foot plateau with extensive views over the Redwood Valley and Lake Mendocino. The winery was founded in 1982 and today produces 5000 cases per year of organically grown varietal and proprietary wines, such as White Blend Chardonnay, Zinfandel, Charbono, Barbera, Petite Sirah, Cabernet Sauvignon and Port.

KORBEL CHAMPAGNE CELLARS

4 miles north of Santa Rosa and 12 miles west of US 101 at 13250 River Rd., Guerneville 95446. (707) 887-2294. Open for tasting daily; May through Sept. 9 a.m. to 5 p.m.; Oct. through Apr. to 4:30 p.m. One-hour tours between 10 a.m. and 3:45 p.m.; call for exact times. Garden tours are offered mid-Apr. through Sept., Tue. through Sun. at 11 a.m. and 3 p.m.

Korbel bears the name of its founders, three brothers who launched the business in the 1870s. Here among the redwoods on the Russian River, the winery and adjoining brandy tower were built as replicas of buildings in the Korbels' native Bohemia. By 1954, when the winery was bought by the Heck family, the Korbel reputation for sparkling wines and brandy was firmly established. In 1993, Korbel's sparkling wine was served at the 1993 Presidential Inaugural events. Tours of the winery include the Korbel history museum, a multimedia presentation on the production of sparkling wine and a walk through the century-old cellars.

LAKE SONOMA WINERY

9 miles west of US 101 at 9990 Dry Creek Rd., Geyserville (mailing address: P.O. Box 781, 95441). (707) 431-1550. Open for tasting daily; Mar. through Oct. 10 a.m. to 5 p.m.; Nov. through Feb. 11 a.m. to 4 p.m. Tours by appointment.

This 10-acre winery produces 3500 cases annually of Merlot, Zinfandel, Late Harvest Zinfandel and Cinsault. A beautiful, 20-mile view of Dry Creek Valley is seen from the veranda surrounding the winery. Gourmet edibles and wine-related items are available in the gift shop. There are wooded picnic facilities for visitors.

LAMBERT BRIDGE WINERY

North of Healdsburg via US 101 at 4085 W. Dry Creek Rd., 95448. (707) 431-9600. Open for tasting daily 10:30 a.m. to 4:30 p.m. Closed major holidays.

Founded in 1975, Lambert Bridge is now celebrating its 20th vintage year. Located in the heart of Dry Creek Valley, the exterior resembles a wooden barn. Inside, the tasting room features a wine-stained tasting bar made from oak casks, and a fireplace. The winery produces 12,000 cases annually of Chardonnay, Fumé, Merlot, Cabernet Sauvignon, Pinot Noir and Zinfandel. A gift shop and picnic facilities are available for visitors.

LANDMARK VINEYARDS

10 miles east of Santa Rosa at junction of SR 12 to 101 Adobe Canyon Rd., Kenwood 95452. (707) 833-1164, (800) 452-6365. Open for tasting daily 10 a.m. to 4:30 p.m.; tours by appointment.

The winery's early California mission-style building has a fountain in the central courtyard, and the six acres of landscaped grounds include a pond and picnic facilities. Landmark Vineyards is California's oldest exclusively Chardonnay winery and currently produces about 20,000 cases per year.

LANGTRY & GUENOC ESTATE VINEYARDS & WINERY

6 miles southeast of Middletown at 21000 Butts Canyon Rd. (mailing address: P.O. Box 1146, 95461). (707) 987-9127 tasting room; (707) 987-2385. Open for tasting and tours Thur. through Sun. 10 a.m. to 4:30 p.m.

The Guenoc Valley was once the domain of Lillie Langtry, a popular 19th-century actress, and today her portrait graces the winery's labels. The massive winery is built on a hilltop overlooking Langtry's restored ranch house. The Magoon family has planted a vineyard on 300 of their estate's 23,000 acres; production is now 100,000 cases annually. Chardonnay, Petite Sirah, Sauvignon Blanc and a red Meritage blend are among the varietal wines produced. Concerts are held periodically at the historic Langtry House. The winery offers a picnic area and a gift shop for visitors. See Annual Events for Langtry House tour in May.

LAZY CREEK VINEYARDS
North of Philo off SR 128 (mailing address: P.O. Box 176, 95466). (707) 895-3623. Open for tasting and tours by appointment only. Closed Dec. 25.

During his restaurant career, Hans Kobler grew increasingly disappointed that no one was making the kind of wines he enjoyed most, so when he and his wife Teresia began planning their move from the city, he chose a location where he could realize his dream of crafting Alsatian-style Gewürztraminer, in addition to Pinot Noir and Chardonnay. Lazy Creek was the third bonded winery in the Anderson Valley, and production is 4000 cases per year. There is a one-lane dirt road leading to the winery.

LONG VINEYARDS
Mailing address: P.O. Box 50, St. Helena 94574. (707) 963-2496. No tasting; tours by appointment.

Terraced vineyards, period buildings and a modern winery are situated on Pritchard Hill. Soil, climate and care produce 3000 cases annually of Chardonnay, Sauvignon Blanc, Riesling and Cabernet Sauvignon; the small output precludes tasting.

LOUIS M. MARTINI
1 mile south of St. Helena at 254 St. Helena Hwy. S. (mailing address: SR 29, P.O. Box 112, 94574). (707) 963-2736, (800) 321-WINE. Open for tasting and tours daily 10 a.m. to 4:30 p.m. Tasting fee for reserve wines and library selections.

Louis M. Martini built his winery in 1933. Today the family's third generation is building on the traditions of their ancestors. More than 75 percent of the wine comes from the 1000 acres of Martini vineyards in the Napa-Sonoma regions, and the grapes are brought here for crushing, fermenting and aging in the vast assortment of wood cooperage. Martini makes three lines of a large number of varietal wines. The gift shop has a wide array of food products, gifts and cookbooks. Picnic tables are available in the shady "Martini Park."

MARKHAM VINEYARDS
2812 N. St. Helena Hwy., St. Helena (mailing address: P.O. Box 636, 94574). (707) 963-5292. Open for tasting daily 10 a.m. to 5 p.m. Tours by appointment.

Markham is Napa County's fourth-oldest, continuously operated winery, and its roots go back to the days of the California Gold Rush. Jean Laurent, a native of Bordeaux, France, had come for the lure of gold, and not striking it rich, went back to working the land. He discovered that growing grapes was natural to this area, and in 1874 he purchased some land and founded a winery. In 1988 the winery and vineyard were purchased by Mercian, Inc., Japan's largest and oldest wine company. Three vineyards provide grapes for producing Markham's varietals, with annual production of 150,000 cases. Pools, fountains and more than 80 kinds of plants grace the entrance of the winery; the new visitor center includes a gift shop.

MARK WEST ESTATE WINERY
11 miles northwest of Santa Rosa off River Rd. at 7010 Trenton-Healdsburg Rd., Forestville 95436. (707) 544-4813. Open for tasting daily 10 a.m. to 5:30 p.m.

Located atop a knoll in the heart of the Russian River Valley, the winery produces Chardonnay, dry Gewürztraminer and Pinot Noir, utilizing organically grown grapes aged in small French cooperage. Visitors are welcome to visit the natural pond, a greenhouse of carnivorous plants and the gift shop.

Matanzas Creek Winery

Lilac fields and ornamental grasses provide a colorful landscape around Matanzas Creek Winery.

acres of vines and an award-winning landscaped garden that is filled with more than 4500 lavender plants and specimens of ornamental grasses. Production consists of Chardonnay, Merlot and Sauvignon Blanc, as well as a variety of wines available only in the tasting room. A rotating art exhibit of works by local artists is featured in the tasting room.

MAYACAMAS
10 miles west of SR 29 at 1155 Lokoya Rd., Napa 94558. (707) 224-4030. Open for tasting and tours by appointment only.

Mayacamas was founded high on the slopes of Mount Veeder in 1889 by John Fisher, a professional sword engraver and pickle merchant. He sold the winery after the turn of the century, and thereafter the winery changed hands several times. Robert and Elinor Travers have owned the property since 1968. They have concentrated on the production of renowned Cabernet Sauvignon and Chardonnay wines made primarily from Mayacamas-grown grapes; they also produce Sauvignon Blanc, Merlot and Pinot Noir.

MAZZOCCO VINEYARDS
5 miles north of Healdsburg off US 101 at 1400 Lytton Springs Rd. (mailing address: P.O. Box 49, 95448). (707) 431-8159. Open for tasting daily 10 a.m. to 4:30 p.m.; tours by appointment.

Thomas Mazzocco founded his winery in 1985 in the rolling hills between the Alexander and Dry Creek valleys. Winemaker Phyllis Zouzounis vinifies Merlot, Cabernet Sauvignon, Chardonnay, a blended wine, and an unfined and unfiltered Zinfandel available only at the winery. The rosebush-lined driveway leads to the tasting room, which overlooks a small pond.

MARTINI & PRATI, INC.
7 miles west of Santa Rosa at 2191 Laguna Rd., 95401. (707) 823-2404; FAX (707) 829-8662. Open for tasting daily 11 a.m. to 4 p.m. Closed Jan. 1, Easter, Thanksgiving and Dec. 25.

One of Sonoma County's oldest wineries, it has been in operation since 1881. Production includes Chardonnay, Cabernet Sauvignon, Pinot Noir and Zinfandel.

MATANZAS CREEK WINERY
5 miles southeast of Santa Rosa at 6097 Bennett Valley Rd., 95404. (707) 528-6464. Open for tasting and tours Mon. through Sat. 10 a.m. to 4 p.m., Sun. noon to 4 p.m.

Founded in 1976, Matanzas Creek Winery is located on 215 acres in the northern Sonoma Valley. This modern winemaking facility is surrounded by 55

THE MEEKER VINEYARD
9711 W. Dry Creek Rd., Healdsburg 95448. (707) 431-2148. Open for tasting daily 10 a.m. to 4:30 p.m.

The Meeker Vineyard is a small, family owned vineyard producing Cabernet and Chardonnay. They are also known as premier producers of Zinfandel.

MELIM MAACAMA CREEK WINERY
15001 Chalk Hill Rd., Healdsburg, 95448. (707) 433-4774. Open Sat. and Sun. 10 a.m. to 4 p.m.; self-guided tours only.

Thanks to vintners, growers and county organizations, many wineries are clearly marked and easy to find. Others preserve their seclusion by blending into the countryside.

In 1972, Clifford Melim planted vines on 20 acres of undeveloped hillside in the Alexander Valley. The estate is now 80 acres of rolling hills bounded by Maácama Creek, a tributary of the Russian River. Melim produces 8000 cases of Chardonnay and Cabernet Sauvignon, aged in French and American oak barrels. There are picnic facilities for visitors.

MERRYVALE VINEYARDS AT SUNNY ST. HELENA WINERY
1000 Main St., St. Helena 94574. (707) 963-7777. Open for tasting daily 10 a.m. to 5:30 p.m. Component seminar Sat. at 10 a.m.; reservations required. Tours by appointment. $3 fee applied towards purchase.

Founded in 1983, the goal at Merryvale has always been to produce world-class wines from grapes grown in Napa Valley's finest vineyards. Today, wine-maker Bob Levy produces more than 35,000 cases per year of award-winning premium and ultra-premium wines. Wine-related gifts and collectibles are available for purchase.

MICHEL SCHLUMBERGER BENCHLAND WINE ESTATE
4155 Wine Creek Rd., Healdsburg 95448. (707) 433-7427; FAX (707) 433-0444. Open for guided tours daily, by appointment at 11 a.m. and 2 p.m.

This 15-year-old wine estate was found-ed in the 1970s by an adventurous Swiss, Jean-Jacques Michel, and his partner, Ridgely Bullock. Michel found that the land reminded him of the prime wine-growing regions of France. In 1985 a winery was built in California Mission and Moorish style. The winery now produces 18,000 cases of Merlot, Chardonnay and Cabernet Sauvignon under the Domaine Michel label.

MILANO WINERY
14594 S. US 101, Hopland 95449. (707) 744-1396, (800) 564-2582. Open for

tasting daily 10 a.m. to 5 p.m. Tours by appointment only.

Milano Winery is owned and operated by the Milone family, whose involvement with the wine industry spans four generations. In the early 1900s grower Vincenzo Milone settled in Hopland, where the southern Mendocino County countryside reminded him of his home in Brindisi, Italy. In 1976 his grandson, Jim Milone, began converting the hop kiln into a winery. Estate-grown production is about 4000 cases annually of Chardonnay, Cabernet Sauvignon and Zinfandel. Visitors are welcome to use the picnic area.

MILL CREEK VINEYARDS
1401 Westside Rd., Healdsburg (mailing address: P.O. Box 758, 95448). (707) 431-2121. Open for tasting daily 11 a.m. to 5 p.m. Short tours and educational talks by appointment.

A beautifully landscaped, wheelchair-accessible tasting room is complete with working water wheel and mill pond. There is a 3,000-square-foot picnic deck overlooking the Dry Creek Valley. Call for special monthly activities.

MONT ST. JOHN CELLARS
3 miles southwest of Napa off SR 12 at 5400 Old Sonoma Rd., 94559. (707) 255-8864. Open for tasting daily 10 a.m. to 5 p.m. Tours by appointment only.

In 1971 grower and winemaker Louis Bartolucci and his son Andrea acquired 160 acres of vineyard land in the Carneros region. The estate's Madonna Vineyard is well known for its Pinot Noir and Chardonnay grapes; also produced are Cabernet Sauvignon, Riesling and Gewürztraminer. A gift shop and picnic facilities are available for visitors.

MONTICELLO VINEYARDS
5 miles north of Napa off SR 29 and Oak Knoll Ave. at 4242 Big Ranch Rd., 94558. (707) 253-2802, (800) 743-6668. Open

for tasting daily 10 a.m. to 4:30 p.m; tours at 10:30 a.m., 12:30 and 2:30 p.m.

The vineyards at Monticello were planted in 1970, and a modern winery was built in 1982. Annual production is about 20,000 cases of Chardonnay, Cabernet Sauvignon, Merlot and Pinot Noir, and when weather permits, a late-harvest Sémillon. The hospitality center, built in 1984, resembles Thomas Jefferson's home in Virginia, reflecting founder Jay Corley's admiration for one of our country's first wine and food enthusiasts. A shaded picnic grove is available for visitors.

MUMM NAPA VALLEY
2 miles north of Oakville Crossroad at 8445 Silverado Tr., Napa (mailing address: P.O. Drawer 500, Rutherford 94573, 94558). (707) 942-3434. Open for tasting and tours daily Nov. through Apr. 1 from 10 a.m. to 5 p.m.; rest of year 10:30 a.m. to 6 p.m. Nov. through Feb. comprehensive tours offered on the hour with last tour at 3 p.m.; rest of year at 4 p.m. $3.50 to $7.50 tasting fee includes several wines.

This *méthode champenoise* sparkling wine facility is the final result of a project begun in 1979 by Champagne Mumm et Cie. and Joseph E. Seagram & Sons. The gift shop sells wine and wine-related items.

MURPHY-GOODE ESTATE WINERY
5 miles southeast of Geyserville at 4001 SR 128 (mailing address: P.O. Box 158, 95441). (707) 431-7644. Open for tasting 10:30 a.m. to 4:30 p.m. Closed major holidays.

Tim Murphy and Dale Goode teamed up with wine marketer Dave Ready to develop this 150-acre, family estate winery in Sonoma County's prestigious Alexander Valley. The porous, well-drained soils of the valley and hillside estate produce grapes for Chardonnay and Reserve Chardonnay, Merlot, Fumé

Blanc and Reserve Fumé, Cabernet Sauvignon and Pinot Blanc. There is a gift shop for visitors.

NAVARRO VINEYARDS
3 miles north of Philo at 5601 SR 128 (mailing address: P.O. Box 47, 95466). (707) 895-3686. Open for tasting daily; Jun. through Aug. 10 a.m. to 6 p.m., Nov. through Feb. to 5 p.m. Tours by appointment.

The winery facilities at Navarro Vineyards are located in a refurbished old barn, flanked by stainless steel fermenters and backed by 80 acres of terraced vineyards. Ted Bennett produces 22,000 cases per year of premium Riesling, Cabernet Sauvignon, Chardonnay, Pinot Noir and the house specialty, Gewürztraminer. Picnic facilities are available for visitors.

NEWLAN VINEYARDS & WINERY
5225 Solano Ave., Napa 94558. (707) 257-2399. Open for tasting and tours by appointment, Mon. through Sat. 10 a.m. to 4 p.m.

Established in 1981, this small winery produces estate-bottled Chardonnay, Pinot Noir, Cabernet Sauvignon and Sauvignon Blanc from its Napa Valley vineyard.

NEWTON VINEYARD
2555 Madrona Ave., St. Helena (mailing address: P.O. Box 540, 94574). (707) 963-9000. No tasting; tours Fri. by appointment.

Thirteen years after he founded Sterling Vineyards, Peter Newton sold the operation and turned his attention toward a new challenge. The winery that now bears his name stands amid 560 acres of spectacularly terraced vineyards on the steep slopes of Spring Mountain above St. Helena. The winery produces Chardonnay, Cabernet Sauvignon and Merlot in the modern underground cellars and cave.

NICHELINI WINERY
11 miles east of Rutherford at junction of SR 128; 2950 Sage Canyon Rd., St. Helena 94574. (707) 963-0717. Open for tasting and self-guided tours by appointment; May to Nov., Sat. and Sun. 10 a.m. to 6 p.m.; Nov. to May, Mon. through Fri. to 5 p.m.

Nichelini Vineyard was founded in 1890 by Swiss-Italian immigrant Anton Nichelini. Today, four of his grandchildren own and operate the winery he built, making Cabernet, Petite Sirah (Sauvignon Vert), Merlot and Zinfandel. Visitors are welcome to picnic under the 80-year-old walnut trees.

NIEBAUM-COPPOLA ESTATE WINERY
1460 Niebaum Ln., Rutherford 94573. (707) 963-9099. Open for tasting daily 10 a.m. to 5 p.m. $5 tasting fee.

Niebaum-Coppola's history spans more than a century and involves two individuals who were successful in professions very different from winemaking. Gustave Niebaum, a Finnish sea captain, made his fortune on furs from Alaska, and in 1887 he founded Inglenook. In 1978, filmmaker Francis Ford Coppola founded a winery, producing a red table wine blended from Cabernet Franc, Cabernet Sauvignon, Chardonnay and Merlot; it was first released in 1984. In 1995 Coppola also acquired the Inglenook winery and chateau, which had not been used for winemaking in two decades; he plans to make wines there as well.

OBESTER WINERY
¼ mile south at 9200 SR 128, Philo 95466. (707) 895-3814. Open for tasting daily 10 a.m. to 5 p.m. Tours by appointment only.

Unable to expand their Half Moon Bay facility because of zoning restrictions, Paul and Sandy Obester purchased 85 acres in the Anderson Valley, where seven acres are currently planted to equal parts Chardonnay, Gewürztraminer and

Pinot Noir. Obester also produces Sauvignon Blanc, Johannisberg Riesling, Sangiovese, Zinfandel, nonalcoholic and varietal grape juices and other gourmet foods. Production is approximately 10,000 cases annually. Picnic tables and a gazebo are available for picnickers.

PARDUCCI WINE CELLARS
3 miles north at 501 Parducci Rd., Ukiah 95482. (707) 463-5350. Open for tasting daily 9 a.m. to 5 p.m.; 30-minute guided tours from 10 a.m. to 3 p.m. (last tour at 3 p.m.).

The winery, founded in 1931 by Adolph Parducci, has placed increasing emphasis on the production of premium varietal wines. The winemaking philosophy allows grapes to become wine with as little human intervention as possible. A gravity-flow system eliminates the need for pumping—"settling out" is preferred to filtering, and handling is kept to a minimum. The wines can be sampled in the tasting room, located in front of the cellars. A gift shop, art gallery, and picnic facilities are available for visitors.

PASTORI WINERY
23189 Geyserville Ave., Cloverdale 95425. (707) 857-3418. Open for tasting daily 9 a.m. to 5 p.m. Closed Jan. 1, Easter, Thanksgiving and Dec. 25.

The Pastori family's microwinery, established in 1975, produces 1000 cases of Red Zinfandel, Chardonnay, White Zinfandel and Burgundy.

PEJU PROVINCE
8466 St. Helena Hwy., Rutherford (mailing address: P.O. Box 478, 94573). (707) 963-3600. Open for tasting daily 10 a.m. to 6 p.m.; self-guided tours. $2 tasting fee refundable with purchase.

Anthony Peju crushed his first vintage in 1982, and he now produces 8000 cases per year of estate Cabernet Sauvignon, Chardonnay and Meritage. He also makes Carnival, a proprietary French Colombard; Karma, a dry rosé; and late harvest wines. The two-level winery, a design that was the result of a competition between four leading California architects, was completed in 1991. An exhibit of marble sculpture by Northern California artist Welton Rotz is on display. A stone walkway leads through a flower garden past a wishing well. A number of wine-related books and gifts are available in the gift shop.

A wishing well lies at the center of an extensive rock and flower garden that welcomes visitors to Peju Province Winery.

PEPPERWOOD SPRINGS VINEYARDS

6 miles west of Philo on SR 128 at 1200 Holmes Ranch Rd. (mailing address: P.O. Box 2, 95466). (707) 895-2920. Open by appointment 11 a.m. to 5:30 p.m.; tasting Mon. through Fri.; tours Sat. and Sun.

Situated on a ridge at about 1600 feet, the winery has a spectacular view of the Anderson Valley. Pepperwood Springs produces 1800 cases of Sauvignon Blanc, Chardonnay and Pinot Noir. There are picnic facilities for visitors.

PINE RIDGE WINERY

5901 Silverado Tr., Napa 94558. (707) 252-9777, (800) 575-9777. Open for tasting daily; May through Sep. 11 a.m. to 5 p.m., Oct. through Apr. to 4 p.m. Tours by appointment at 10:15 a.m., 1 and 3 p.m. $3 tasting fee includes souvenir glass.

Pine Ridge is located in a small fold in the hilly Stags Leap area of the Napa Valley. Fifty acres of estate vineyards, plus 150 acres throughout the Napa Valley, provide the finest of fruit for an annual 65,000-case output of Merlot, Chardonnay, Chenin Blanc and Cabernet Sauvignon wines. Visitors are welcome to picnic.

PLAM VINEYARDS & WINERY

1 mile south at 6200 Washington St., Yountville 94599. (707) 944-1102; FAX (707) 963-1727. Open for tasting and tours by appointment, Mon. through Sat. 9 a.m. to 6 p.m., and Sun. 11 a.m. to 6 p.m.

This small stone winery is nestled in a quiet bend on Hopper Creek and sheltered by majestic old oak trees. The winery produces Sauvignon Blanc, Cabernet Sauvignon, Merlot and Chardonnay. Visitors are welcome to use the picnic facilities.

PRAGER WINERY

1 mile south at 1281 Lewelling Ln., St. Helena 94574. (707) 963-PORT. Open

for tasting and sales daily 10 a.m. to 4:30 p.m.; tours by appointment.

Jim Prager and his family crushed their first vintage in 1980. The fermentation and press room is located in a century-old carriage house, while a similar new facility houses the barrel aging cellar and tasting room. Prager vinifies atypical medium-dry ports, along with Cabernet Sauvignon and Chardonnay varietals.

PRESTON VINEYARDS

8 miles northwest at 9282 W. Dry Creek Rd., Healdsburg 95448. (707) 433-3372. Open for tasting daily 11 a.m. to 4:30 p.m.

Preston Vineyards is a family owned, 125-acre wine estate in Sonoma County's Dry Creek Valley. It specializes in Zinfandel, Sauvignon Blanc, Rhône-style wines and other unusual varietals. The Prestons are natural-method growers; one-third of the acres are certified organic. Products under development include olive oil, cured olives and bread. Visitors can use the boccie courts and picnic grounds, and there are friendly cats to pet in the Mediterranean-style kitchen.

QUIVIRA VINEYARDS

5½ miles northwest at 4900 W. Dry Creek Rd., Healdsburg 95448. (707) 431-8333. Open for tasting 10 a.m. to 4:30 p.m. Tours by appointment only. Closed major holidays.

Quivira, named after the mythical civilization that enticed 16th- and 17th-century explorers, was founded in 1981 and now produces 20,000 cases per year. Zinfandel and Sauvignon Blanc are the house specialties, with Cabernet Sauvignon added in the fall of 1990. The wines are made in a modern cedar and redwood building on the west side of Dry Creek Valley. Shaded picnic facilities overlook the valley.

RAVENSWOOD

18701 Gehricke Rd., Sonoma 95476. (707) 938-1960. Open for tasting daily 10 a.m. to 4:30 p.m. Tours by appointment, mornings only.

Ravenswood winery was founded in Sonoma in 1976. Traditional methods are used for vinifying grapes grown in Napa and Sonoma counties. Production of 90,000 cases per year includes Zinfandel—the winery's hallmark—and Cabernet Sauvignon, Merlot and Chardonnay. There is a picnic area for visitors. Weekend barbecues are held during the summer on a first-come, first-served basis.

RAYMOND VINEYARD AND CELLAR
849 Zinfandel Ln., St. Helena 94574. (800) 525-2659. Open for tasting daily 10 a.m. to 4 p.m. Tours by appointment.

The Raymonds began this family enterprise in 1971 with the purchase of a 90-acre estate. The estate vineyard has now expanded to include 250 acres in the Jameson Canyon region of Napa Valley and 300 acres in Monterey County. The state-of-the-art winery and barrel-aging buildings were completed in 1993.

Production is currently 175,000 cases per year of Chardonnay, Merlot, Cabernet Sauvignon, Sauvignon Blanc, Pinot Noir and Red Meritage.

ROBERT KEENAN WINERY
4 miles northwest at 3660 Spring Mountain Rd., St. Helena 94574. (707) 963-9177. Open for tasting and tours by appointment only.

This winery dates to 1904, but when it was purchased by Robert Keenan in 1974, the vineyards had reverted to forest and only the stone walls of the original structure were still standing. The building has been handsomely restored and outfitted with new oak barrels. Production is limited to Chardonnay, Merlot, Cabernet Sauvignon and a limited production of Cabernet Franc.

ROBERT MONDAVI WINERY
7801 St. Helena Hwy., Oakville (mailing address: SR 29, P.O. Box 106, 94562). (707) 226-1335. Open daily; May through Oct. 9 a.m. to 5 p.m., Nov. through Apr. 9 a.m. to 5:30 p.m. Guided

Although all winemaking begins in the vineyard, tours usually focus on processes inside the winery. At Robert Mondavi Winery, visitors get a close look at the vines.

tours with complimentary tasting; reservations recommended.

In 1966 Robert Mondavi left the Charles Krug Winery, which his family has owned since 1943, to establish his own business. Architect Cliff May was commissioned to design the graceful, Mission-style building, and Mondavi outfitted it with oak cooperage and modern equipment. Zinfandel, Merlot, Moscato d'Oro, Cabernet Sauvignon, Fumé Blanc and Chardonnay are now produced; Brut Reserve and Brut Chardonnay Reserve sparkling wines are also produced and are for sale only at the winery. Reserve wines may be sampled in the To-Kalon Room for a fee. An art gallery and gift shop are available for visitors. During July, the winery sponsors Saturday evening concerts with wine and cheese tasting at intermission. Across the street is Opus One Winery, jointly owned by the Robert Mondavi Corporation and the family of Baron Phillipe de Rothschild; open by appointment only, (707) 944-9442.

ROBERT PECOTA WINERY

2½ miles north at 3299 Bennett Ln., Calistoga (mailing address: P.O. Box 303, 94515). (707) 942-6625. Open for tasting and tours by appointment only.

After a career in San Francisco as a coffee roaster and tea packer, Robert Pecota founded a winery in 1978. North of Calistoga on the Napa Valley floor, at the foot of Mt. St. Helena, his replanted 45-year-old vineyard produces Sauvignon Blanc, Cabernet Sauvignon, Merlot, Gamay Beaujolais and Muscat Blanc. Each of the three principal varietals is dedicated to one of Pecota's children.

ROBERT PEPI WINERY

7 miles south of St. Helena on SR 29 at 7585 St. Helena Hwy., Oakville 94562. (707) 944-2807. Open for tasting daily 10:30 a.m. to 4:30 p.m. $2 tasting fee includes glass.

Located on top of a knoll overlooking Napa Valley, the winery was built in 1991 by Robert Pepi and is owned by Kendall-Jackson Winery. It produces 25,000 cases of Sauvignon Blanc, Sangiovese, Chardonnay and Cabernet Sauvignon.

ROBERT SINSKEY VINEYARDS

South of Yountville Cross Rd. at 6320 Silverado Tr., Napa 94558. (707) 944-9090. Open for tasting Mar. through Oct., daily 10 a.m. to 4:30 p.m. Call for hours Nov. through Feb. Closed major holidays. Tours by appointment. $3 includes souvenir glass or refund with purchase.

Robert Sinskey Vineyards cover 120 acres in three Carneros locations and the Stags Leap district. Sinskey has become a proven Pinot Noir and Merlot specialist. He and winemaker Jeff Virnig have teamed up to create unique methods of producing Pinot Noir and Merlot. The winery is built of Napa Valley stone, and there is a redwood tasting room.

ROCHE WINERY

On SR 121 near Sears Point Raceway, at 28700 Arnold Dr., Sonoma 95476. (800) 825-9475. Open for tasting daily 10 a.m. to 6 p.m.

A panorama of the Carneros region can be seen from the winery, which produces 3600 cases of Chardonnay and Pinot Noir. Winery dinners hosted by Chef Claude and Gail Jean are a special highlight; call for reservations. There are picnic facilities and a gift shop for visitors.

ROCHIOLI VINEYARDS & WINERY

6 miles southwest of Healdsburg at 6192 Westside Rd., 95448. (707) 433-2305. Open for tasting daily 10 a.m. to 5 p.m. Tours by appointment only.

The Rochiolis have grown grapes in the Russian River Valley since the 1930s, but it wasn't until 1982 that they began vinifying and marketing their own wines. From 100 acres of estate vine-yards, they now produce 5000 cases per year of Sauvignon Blanc, Chardonnay, Pinot Noir, Gewürztraminer and Cabernet Sauvignon. The tasting room features work by local artists, and visi-tors are welcome to picnic.

RODNEY STRONG VINEYARDS

12 miles north of Santa Rosa at 11455 Old Redwood Hwy., Windsor (mailing address: P.O. Box 368, 95492). (707) 431-1533, (800) 678-4763. Open for tasting daily 10 a.m. to 5 p.m. Tours daily at 11 a.m., 1 and 3 p.m.

Rodney Strong was one of the first to name vineyards on wine labels, and six of his estate-grown varietals carry vine-yard designations. The building, designed by architect Craig Roland (a student of Frank Lloyd Wright), houses a skylit tasting bar, a gift shop, the win-ery and cellar. A walkway encircling the tasting room allows visitors to view the storage and aging area below; the lower level of the winery is designed so that winemaking operations take place in the center of the building, beneath the tast-ing room, and storage and aging takes place in the wings. Vertical tastings are offered on Saturday and Sunday, and more frequently in summer. A picnic area is available.

ROEDERER ESTATE

5 miles north of Philo at 4501 SR 128 (mailing address: P.O. Box 67, 95466). (707) 895-2288. Open for tasting daily 11 a.m. to 5 p.m. Tours by appointment only.

Champagne Louis Roederer of France spent two years in search of a suitable California location before purchasing 580 acres of land in the Anderson Valley. The vineyards were planted in 1982, and the first sparkling wine was released six years later.

ROUND HILL WINERY

1680 Silverado Tr., St. Helena 94574. (707) 963-9503, 963-5251. Open for

retail sales daily 10 a.m. to 4:30 p.m. No tasting or tours.

The Round Hill winery, a stockholder-owned operation, was founded in 1977 and moved to its present facility a decade later. Wines are produced from grapes grown in the owners' vineyards and at other selected sites. At present, Round Hill makes 375,000 cases annual-ly of Cabernet Sauvignon, Chardonnay, Merlot, Sauvignon Blanc and Zinfandel.

S. ANDERSON VINEYARD

473 Yountville Crossroad, Napa 94599. (800) 428-2259. Open daily; tasting from 10 a.m. to 5 p.m. Tours at 10:30 a.m. and 2:30 p.m.

A producer of world-class champagnes, Chardonnays and Cabernet, S. Ander-son Vineyard is situated on beautiful knolls and surrounded by flower-filled gardens. Founded by the Anderson fami-ly in 1971, they now farm 120 acres in the Stags Leap and Carneros districts of Napa Valley. After 10 years as grape growers, the Andersons produced their first wine under the S. Anderson label to outstanding critical acclaim in 1980. Their wines have brought home more than 36 Gold Medals in recent years and have been served to six U.S. Presidents.

SAINTSBURY

4 miles southwest off SR 12/121 at 1500 Los Carneros Ave., Napa 94559. (707) 252-0592; FAX (707) 252-0595. Open for tasting and tours Mon. through Fri. by appointment. Closed Sat., Sun., Jan. 1, Easter, Thanksgiving and Dec. 25.

Saintsbury wines were first made in 1981, and a modern winery was complet-ed in the Napa Valley's Carneros district in 1983. Grapes are purchased from local vineyards and are carefully processed and aged in French oak cooperage. The own-ers/winemakers have devoted their efforts to Burgundian varietals: at pre-sent, 40,000 cases of Chardonnay and Pinot Noir are produced annually.

SAUSAL WINERY

7 miles northeast at 7370 SR 128, Healdsburg 95448. (707) 433-2285; FAX (707) 433-5136. Open for tasting daily 10 a.m. to 4 p.m.

Now in its third generation of wine-making in the Alexander Valley, the Demostene family purchased Sausal Ranch in 1956, when the 125 acres were planted to prunes, apples and grapes. Leo Demostene's dream of a winery was brought to fruition by his four children in 1973. They now annually produce 10,000 cases of three Zinfandels: Cabernet Sauvignon, White Zinfandel and a white proprietary blend.

SCHARFFENBERGER CELLARS

8501 SR 128, Philo 95466. (707) 895-2065. Open for tasting daily 11 a.m. to 5 p.m. Winery open by appointment only.

Established in 1981 by John Scharffenberger, the winery and tasting room are located on 685 acres in downtown Philo. This *méthode champenoise* sparkling wine facility vinifies Chardonnay and Pinot Noir from Anderson Valley grapes. The winery produces 32,000 cases annually. The visitor center, located just north of Philo, has picnic facilities available.

SCHRAMSBERG VINEYARDS

5 miles north of St. Helena off SR 29 at to 1400 Schramsberg Rd., Calistoga 94515. (707) 942-4558. Open for tours and tasting daily by appointment at 10 and 11:30 a.m., 1 and 2:30 p.m. Tasting fee $6.50 for three current releases.

Founded in 1862 by Jacob Schram, Schramsberg was the first hillside winery in the Napa Valley. In 1965 Jack and Jamie Davies purchased the historic site and set out to produce *méthode champenoise* sparkling wines; they now produce six styles of vintage champagne with an annual production of about 35,000 cases.

SEBASTIANI VINEYARDS

389 4th St. E., Sonoma (mailing address: P.O. Box AA, 95476). (707) 938-5532, (800) 888-5532. Open for tasting daily 10 a.m. to 5 p.m.; tours between 10:30 a.m. and 4 p.m. Closed major holidays.

Sebastiani is one of California's oldest family wineries. In 1904 it produced its first wine, a Zinfandel; since then, the list has been expanded to include a full range of table and dessert wines. The winery features a large collection of hand-carved oak barrels. A picnic area is located adjacent to the winery. There are a variety of refrigerated deli items for sale, and a gift shop for visitors.

SEGHESIO VINEYARDS & WINERY

South of Dry Creek Rd. and east off US 101 at 14730 Grove St., Healdsburg 95448. (707) 433-3579. Open for tasting by appointment only, Mon. through Fri. 8 a.m. to 5 p.m.

In 1895, Eduardo Seghesio began a family tradition; he and his wife Angela settled in Sonoma County's Alexander Valley, and drew on their Italian wine heritage by planting grapes and opening a winery in 1902. The third and fourth generations now manage the operation and produce Chardonnay, Cabernet Sauvignon, Sauvignon Blanc, Pinot Noir, Sangiovese and Old Vine Zinfandel.

SEQUOIA GROVE VINEYARDS

1 mile south of Rutherford at 8338 St. Helena Hwy. (SR 29), Napa 94558. (707) 944-2945. Open for tasting daily 11 a.m. to 5 p.m.; tours at 2 and 4 p.m. Closed Jan. 1, Easter, Thanksgiving and Dec. 25. $3 tasting fee includes souvenir glass

Several massive redwood trees, seemingly out of place on the Napa Valley floor, tower over the winery. Grapes are grown on the 24-acre vineyard surrounding the winery, which is housed in a refurbished barn. The Allen family produces 25,000

The modern stone facade of Sebastiani Vineyards, one of California's oldest family wineries, dates to 1904.

cases each year of Chardonnay and Cabernet Sauvignon.

SHAFER VINEYARDS

¾ mile south of Yountville Crossroad at 6154 Silverado Tr., Napa 94558. (707) 944-2877; FAX (707) 944-9454. Open for tasting and 30-minute tours Mon. through Fri. by appointment.

John Shafer, his wife and four children moved from Chicago to the Stags Leap District in 1972 and began the arduous task of replanting 30 acres of hillside vineyards. Their winery was built in 1979 against the foothills in a small valley off the Silverado Trail. The local microclimate was responsible for the family's decision to emphasize Cabernet Sauvignon; Chardonnay, Merlot and Sangiovese are also produced. The vineyards have grown to 142 acres on their estate and in the Oak Knoll and Carneros regions of the Napa Valley.

SILVER OAK CELLARS

From US 101 exit Canyon Rd., take Chianti Rd. 3 miles north to 24625 Chianti Rd., Geyserville (mailing address: P.O. Box 558, 95441). (707) 857-3562. Open for tasting Mon. through Fri. 9 a.m. to 4:30 p.m., Sat. 10 a.m. to 4:30 p.m.; tours by appointment Mon. through Fri. at 1:30 p.m. $5 tasting fee.

Silver Oak Cellars, founded in 1972, is dedicated to the exclusive production of the best Cabernet Sauvignon wines. All the wines are made from 100 percent Cabernet Sauvignon grapes, aged over 30 months in American oak barrels and then cellared for about 15 months.

SILVER OAK WINE CELLARS

1 mile east of Oakville at 915 Oakville Crossroad (mailing address: P.O. Box 414, 94562). (707) 944-8808. Open for tasting Mon. through Fri. 9 a.m. to 4:30 p.m., and Sat. 10 a.m. to 4:30 p.m.; tours Mon. through Fri. by appointment at 1:30 p.m. $5 tasting fee includes souvenir glass or refund with purchase.

Justin Meyer and Ray Duncan founded Silver Oak Cellars in 1972 to produce only one varietal, Cabernet Sauvignon. They obtain their grapes from vineyards in the Napa and Alexander valleys, then oak and age the product five years in the bottle before release.

SILVERADO VINEYARDS
1 mile south of Yountville Crossroad at 6121 Silverado Tr., Napa 94558. (707) 257-1770. Open for tasting daily 11 a.m. to 4:30 p.m. Tours by appointment.

The Walt Disney family purchased their vineyards in the Stags Leap district in the 1970s and christened them Silverado, inspired by a short book written by Robert Louis Stevenson about his Napa Valley experiences. In 1981, the family began constructing a winery. Winemaker John Stuart produces 80,000 cases per year of Cabernet, Chardonnay, Merlot, Sangiovese and Sauvignon Blanc; these wines may be sampled in the tasting room. Fine art displays change periodically in the hall leading from the tasting room to a large window overlooking the Napa Valley.

SIMI WINERY, INC.
1 mile north of Healdsburg at 16275 Healdsburg Ave. (mailing address: P.O. Box 698, 95448). (707) 433-6981. Open daily; tasting 10 a.m. to 4:30 p.m. Tours at 11 a.m., 1 and 3 p.m.

Founded in 1876, Simi is now known for producing complex, elegant wines and for innovative viticultural processes and winemaking practices. All wines are available for tasting in the visitor center. There is also a picnic area for visitors.

SMITH-MADRONE VINEYARDS
6 miles northwest of St. Helena at 4022 Spring Mountain Rd., 94574. (707) 963-2283. Open for tasting and tours by appointment.

The first Smith-Madrone vines were planted in 1972, and the winery was completed six years later. The vineyards now cover about 40 acres and yield nearly 5000 cases of premium Chardonnay, Riesling and Cabernet Sauvignon a year.

SMOTHERS WINERY
9575 SR 12, Kenwood 95452. (707) 833-1010. Tasting room location open daily 10 a.m. to 4:30 p.m.

The winery was founded in 1977 and the present tasting room location opened in 1982. Comedians Dick and Tom Smothers produce Chardonnay and Cabernet Sauvignon from their vineyards in Santa Cruz, Glen Ellen and Sonoma. A gift shop is available for visitors.

SONOMA CREEK WINERY
South of Sonoma via SR 12 to SR 121, at 23355 Millerick Rd., 95476. (707) 938-3031; FAX (707) 938-3424. Open for tasting and guided tours Apr. to Nov., Sat. and Sun. 11 a.m. to 4 p.m.

The Larson family owns this 20,000-case winery which produces Chardonnay, Cabernet Sauvignon, Pinot Noir and Zinfandel. The land of Sonoma Creek has a colorful history dating back to the 1800s. It was used for various enterprises: as a successful dairy operation, for raising Brahma steers and pedigree horses, and staging rodeos. The land was then used for grazing until the grandchildren returned in 1978 to found the organic vineyards and winery.

SONOMA-CUTRER VINEYARDS
4401 Slusser Rd., Windsor 95492. (707) 528-1181. Open for tasting by appointment Mon. through Fri. 8 a.m. to 5 p.m. Tours Jun. through Oct. on Sat. at 11 a.m. and 2 p.m.; Nov. through May, Mon. through Fri. at 2 p.m.

Sonoma-Cutrer is dedicated exclusively to producing estate-bottled Chardonnay. Fruit from several Sonoma County vineyards owned by the winery is hand-harvested and sorted, barrel-fermented, and aged on the lees in French oak.

ST. CLEMENT VINEYARDS
1½ miles north of St. Helena at 2867 N. St. Helena Hwy. (mailing address: P.O. Box 261, 94574). (707) 963-7221. Open for tasting daily 10 a.m. to 4 p.m. Tours by appointment. Closed major holidays. $2 tasting fee refundable with purchase.

The gabled Victorian house at the base of Spring Mountain was built in

1878 by stained glass merchant Fritz H. Rosenbaum. The estate was the eighth bonded winery in Napa Valley. Dr. William Casey bought the property in 1979 and built a modern winery, which was sold to Sapporo Ltd. in 1987. Winemaker Dennis Johns has been at St. Clement since 1980, and current releases include Merlot, Cabernet Sauvignon, Sauvignon Blanc and Chardonnay.

ST. FRANCIS WINERY
8450 Sonoma Hwy., Kenwood 95452. (707) 833-4666. Open for tasting daily 10 a.m. to 4:30 p.m.

In the area known as the "Valley of the Moon" lies the picturesque and historic town of Kenwood, home to St. Francis Winery. The redwood winery is situated on the 100-acre St. Francis estate, originally planted to vines in 1910. The estate was purchased by Joe Martin, a white collar worker turned vine-grower. For eight years he produced and sold his grapes to neighboring wineries. After building an exceptional reputation with his Merlot and Chardonnay grapes, he decided to build his own winery. In 1979 the winery was completed and christened after St. Francis of Assisi, patron saint of the last mission on the California Mission Trail. A gift shop, refrigerated deli items and picnic area are available for visitors.

ST. SUPÉRY VINEYARDS & WINERY
8440 St. Helena Hwy., Rutherford 94573. (707) 963-4507. Open for tasting daily 9:30 a.m. to 4:30 p.m. Tours depart every 30 minutes on Sat. and Sun.; Mon. through Fri. visitors should call ahead. Closed major holidays. $2.50 tasting fee.

In 1982 French businessman Robert Skalli purchased a vineyard property, the Dollarhide Ranch in Pope Valley. In 1986 he acquired more property in the Rutherford Bench area, once owned by Philadelphia clothier Joseph Atkinson and later by French winemaker Edward

St. Supéry. Atkinson's 1882 Queen Anne-style home has been restored to its pre-Prohibition, wine-boom period and is open for tours. The St. Supéry Visitor Center includes a topographic relief map of the Napa Valley and a smelling station where visitors can learn about wine-tasting and its terminology; a vineyard exhibit displays different trellising and pruning methods. Production at St. Supéry includes Chardonnay, Sauvignon Blanc, Merlot and Cabernet Sauvignon, made primarily with grapes from Dollarhide Ranch and the St. Supéry vineyard.

STAG'S LEAP WINE CELLARS
6 miles north of Napa at 5766 Silverado Tr., 94558. (707) 944-2020. Open for tasting daily 10 a.m. to 4 p.m.; tours by appointment.

Stag's Leap Wine Cellars was founded by Warren and Barbara Winiarski in 1972. The well-designed, modern facility sits at the foot of its namesake, a landmark rock outcropping. The winery's superb reputation has supported expansion to 100,000 cases each year of Stag's Leap and Hawk Crest, a lighter style wine. Stag's Leap Wine Cellars specializes in Cabernet Sauvignon, Riesling, Chardonnay, Merlot, Petite Sirah and Sauvignon Blanc.

STERLING VINEYARDS
1 mile south of Calistoga between SR 29 and Silverado Tr. at 1111 Dunaweal Ln. (mailing address: P.O. Box 365, 94515). Accessible only via an aerial tram that shuttles visitors back and forth from the parking area at $6 per person (under age 18, $3). (707) 942-3344, (800) 726-6136. Open for tasting and self-guided tours daily 10:30 a.m. to 4:30 p.m.

Undeniably one of the most magnificent California wineries, Sterling's white monastic buildings rise from a bluff to overlook the Napa Valley. From elevated viewing galleries visitors are guided through the winemaking process via illustrated, interpretive panels. The tasting room, located halfway up the tram route in Sterling Terrace, offers a spectacular view, a picnic area and a selection of wine accessories and gifts. The Three Palms Gallery features local artists.

STONEGATE WINERY

1 mile south at 1183 Dunaweal Ln., Calistoga 94515. (707) 942-6500. Open for tasting daily 10:30 a.m. to 4:30 p.m. Tasting $1.50 on Sat., Sun. and holidays.

Founded in 1973 by James Spaulding and Barbara Spaulding Hageman, Stonegate Winery's goal is to produce exceptional wines from their hillside vineyards in northern Napa Valley. In production are Cabernet Sauvignon, Merlot, Red Reserve, Sauvignon Blanc, Cabernet Franc, Chardonnay and Late Harvest.

STONY HILL VINEYARD

Mailing address: P.O. Box 308, St. Helena 94574. (707) 963-2636. No tasting; tours by appointment.

Perched on a crest of the Mayacamas Mountains above St. Helena is one of the smallest and most prestigious wineries in the Napa Valley. Stony Hill was bonded in 1951, when Fred McCrea began making his estate-bottled varietals in extremely limited quantities. Now winemaker Michael Chelini carries on the tradition. The Stony Hill label appears on three premium white wines—Riesling, Gewürztraminer and Chardonnay—which are sold out as soon as they are released.

SULLIVAN VINEYARDS WINERY

1 mile north of Rutherford at 1090 Galleron Rd. (mailing address: P.O. Box G, 94573). (707) 963-9646, (800) 501-4669; FAX (707) 963-0377. Open for tasting and tours daily by appointment.

Established in 1979 by winemaker Jim Sullivan, the winery produces small amounts of ultra-premium Merlot, Cabernet Sauvignon and a Bordeaux-

style reserve blend called Coeur de Vigne (Heart of the Vineyard).

SUTTER HOME WINERY, INC.

2½ miles south of St. Helena at 277 St. Helena Hwy. S. (mailing address: SR 29, P.O. Box 248, 94574). (707) 963-3104. Open for tasting daily, Jun. through Aug. 9 a.m. to 5:30 p.m.; Sept. through May to 5 p.m.

In 1874 a Swiss-German immigrant named John Thomann established a small winery and distillery. In 1947, Sutter Home was purchased by John and Mario Trinchero, Italian immigrant brothers whose family had long been in the wine industry. Mario's children, Bob, Roger and Vera, now continue the family business. The winery and the gardens have become landmarks in the Napa Valley; the gardens feature more than 800 varieties of plants and an herb garden. Visitors are welcome to visit the garden and browse in the gift shop. A bed and breakfast inn offers accommodations.

TOPOLOS AT RUSSIAN RIVER VINEYARDS

5700 Gravenstein Hwy. N., Forestville (mailing address: SR 116, P.O. Box 358, 95436). Winery (707) 887-1575; restaurant (707) 887-1562. Open for tasting daily 11 a.m. to 5 p.m. Tours by appointment only. Restaurant open daily from Memorial through Labor days; rest of year Wed. through Sun.

Built in 1969, the winery at Russian River Vineyards is modeled after Sonoma County's hop kilns and the old Russian stockade at Fort Ross. The Topolos family took over in 1978 and has expanded the 8000-case-per-year list of wines to include six varietals. Organically grown grapes are used from their 25-acre vineyard, along with those from nearby vineyards. The building also houses a restaurant that serves continental and Greek cuisine.

TRAULSEN VINEYARDS
2250 Lake County Hwy., Calistoga 94515. (707) 942-0283; FAX (707) 942-0403. Open for tasting and tours of winery, vineyard and garden 10 a.m. to 5 p.m.; Jun. through Aug. Thur. through Mon., Nov. through Feb. Fri. to Sun.; also by appointment. Closed Jan. 1, Easter, Jul. 4, Thanksgiving and Dec. 24-25.

John Traulsen, pharmacologist and community pharmacist, began as a home winemaker. He now specializes in Zinfandel. One of Napa Valley's smallest bonded wineries, the stone-faced building is draped in wisteria. Handcrafted redwood doors open to reveal walls lined with three tiers of French oak barrels; there are also a redwood fermenter and a basket press. This wine is one of the hardest to find and most sought-after Zinfandels in the world: handcrafted and aged for 18 months, it may be fined with egg white and then bottle-aged for two or three years. Two acres of vineyards produce 500 cases of estate Zinfandel per year. The gardens contain roses, perennials and sculptures. See Annual Events in May for open house.

TREFETHEN VINEYARDS
3 miles north of Napa off SR 29 at 1160 Oak Knoll Ave. (mailing address: P.O. Box 2460, 94558). (707) 255-7700. Open for tasting daily 10 a.m. to 4:30 p.m. Tours by appointment.

After years of idleness, the massive redwood winery was acquired by the Trefethen family. Surrounding the building are 600 acres of vines, from which the Trefethens make about 75,000 cases annually of their premium varietal wines: Chardonnay, Riesling and Cabernet Sauvignon/Merlot. Two proprietary blends are also vinified in the historical three-floored structure.

TRENTADUE WINERY
3 miles south at 19170 Geyserville Ave., Geyserville 95441. (707) 433-3104; FAX (707) 433-5825. Open for tasting and vineyard tours daily 10 a.m. to 5 p.m. Closed Jan. 1, Thanksgiving and Dec. 25.

Trefethen Vineyards' massive redwood winery was resurrected by the Trefethen family after years of idleness.

Trentadue was established by Leo and Evelyn Trentadue, descendants of Italian families that included several generations of winemakers. Former owners of fruit orchards in the Santa Clara Valley, the development of the Silicon Valley threatened their rural lifestyle. In 1959 the Trentadues purchased a home in the heart of Sonoma County's Alexander Valley. The property contained a sizeable old vineyard, and so began a winemaking odyssey which has resulted in more than two decades of premium wine production. Today Trentadue produces 25,000 cases a year of Petite Sirah, Zinfandel, Old Patch Red (from old vines), Merlot, Sangiovese, Carignane, Merlot Port, Chardonnay and two elegant table wines, Bianco and Saluté & Auguri Rosso. A gift shop, a variety of refrigerated deli items and a picnic area are available for visitors.

TUDAL WINERY
4 miles northwest of St. Helena at 1015 Big Tree Rd., 94574. (707) 963-3947. Open for tasting and tours by appointment.

Arnold and Alma Tudal's family planted 10 acres of Cabernet Sauvignon vines on their property in 1974, and five years later began vinifying the yields. Two thousand cases per year are produced from their estate.

TURNBULL WINE CELLARS
North of Oakville on SR 29 at 8210 St. Helena Hwy. (mailing address: SR 29, Box 29, 94562). (707) 963-5839; FAX (707) 887-6285. Open for tasting and tours by appointment, daily 10 a.m. to 4 p.m.

Founded in 1976 by an architect and an attorney, Johnson Turnbull Vineyards has become known for its Cabernet Sauvignon, which often has a uniquely minty character. The winery was purchased in 1993 by California publisher Patrick O'Dell, who changed the label to Turnbull Wine Cellars and is expanding the facility. A proprietary blend of Sangiovese/Cabernet Sauvignon and a Merlot are also produced.

V. SATTUI WINERY
2 miles south of St. Helena on SR 29 at 1111 White Ln., 94574. (707) 963-7774; FAX (707) 963-4324. Open for tasting and tours of the underground caves daily; Apr. through Oct. 9 a.m. to 6 p.m.; Nov. through Mar. 9 a.m. to 5 p.m.

Sattui winemaking history dates to 1885, when Vittorio founded his business in San Francisco. Great-grandson Daryl Sattui revived the family tradition in the 1970s by building his facility just south of St. Helena. Currently, 13 vintage-dated wines are being produced; these are available only at the sales room and by mail. There is a tree-shaded picnic grove for visitors, and a European-style deli and gift shop are adjacent.

VALLEY OF THE MOON WINERY
7 miles north of Sonoma at 777 Madrone Rd., Glen Ellen 95442. (707) 996-6941; FAX (707) 996-5809. Open daily for tasting; Jan. through Mar. 10 a.m. to 4:30 p.m., Apr. through Dec. to 5 p.m. Closed Jan. 1, Easter, Thanksgiving and Dec. 25.

Set amidst the lush Sonoma Valley, the winery was part of a Mexican land grant before the Civil War. The vineyard was worked by Indian and Chinese laborers; in the late 1800s French vines were added. Then George Hearst acquired it and operated the facility until Prohibition. During World War II, Enrico Parducci, founder of the San Francisco Sausage Company, purchased the site and wine production began again in 1942. Today, the winery is operated by Parducci's son Harry, his wife Rheda, winemaker Harry, Jr., and production manager Ted Watson. Wine production includes Cabernet Sauvignon, Zinfandel, Chardonnay, Symphony, White Zinfandel and Port. In front of the stone tasting room, built in the 1800s, is a giant Laurel Bay tree that is listed on the National Register of

Historic Places. It is estimated to be more than 400 years old and has 13 intertwined stumps. Visitors may visit the gift shop and use the picnic areas.

VIANSA WINERY AND ITALIAN MARKETPLACE
25200 Arnold Dr., Sonoma 95476. (707) 935-4700. *Open for tasting and self-guided tours daily 10 a.m. to 5 p.m.*

This old-world, Italian-style winery, complete with fresco-style handpainted murals, sits on a hilltop with a view of the winery's 90-acre waterfowl preserve and the Sonoma Valley. Production focuses on Italian varietals: Chardonnay

V. Sattui Winery

The grounds of V. Sattui Winery in Napa Valley are perfect for picnicking; their deli has a wide variety of meats, cheeses and breads.

and Cabernet Sauvignon. An extensive selection of Viansa wines and gourmet packaged foods are available. The Italian kitchen's specialties may be experienced in an Italian cafe setting, or under the grape trellis or olive trees.

VICHON WINERY
1½ miles southwest of Oakville at 1595 Oakville Grade (mailing address: P.O. Box 363, 94562). (707) 944-2811. Open for tasting daily 10 a.m. to 4:30 p.m.; tours by appointment.

This winery, owned by the Robert Mondavi family, sits on a leveled site high on the Oakville Grade. The modern, 55,000-case-per-year facility is the source of four wines: Cabernet Sauvignon, Merlot, Chardonnay and a proprietary blend of Sauvignon Blanc and Sémillon. Visitors are welcome to picnic and visit the gift shop.

VILLA MT. EDEN WINERY
8711 Silverado Tr. at SR 128, St. Helena 94574. (707) 963-9100. Open for

American novelist Jack London called Sonoma Valley "The Valley of the Moon." The valley's ethereal qualities are evident here in Glen Ellen.

tasting daily 10 a.m. to 4 p.m. Tours by appointment.

After many years, Villa Mt. Eden Winery outgrew its former location on Oakville Crossroad and moved in temporarily with its sister winery, Conn Creek, on Silverado Trail. With 17 gold medals, Villa Mt. Eden was the top-scoring winery of those entered into 15 major national fairs, according to *Connoisseur's Guide*, having come in first with Cabernet Sauvignon and Chardonnay and second with Pinot Noir. It also makes Grand Reserve and Cellar Select wines. A gift shop is on premises.

VINCENT ARROYO WINERY
Off SR 29 at 2361 Greenwood, Calistoga 94515. (707) 942-6995. Open for tasting daily 10 a.m. to 4:30 p.m.

This 60-acre winery, built in 1984, produces 3000 cases of Cabernet, Chardonnay, Red Blend and Petite Sirah. Picnic facilities are available for visitors. See Annual Events, May.

WEIBEL WINERY
5 miles north of Ukiah at 7051 N. State St., Redwood Valley (mailing address: P.O. Box 367, 95470). (707) 485-0321. Open for tasting daily 9 a.m. to 5 p.m.

The Weibels were pioneers who brought a passion for winemaking from their native Switzerland, and today they have one of the largest vineyard holdings in Mendocino. In 1945 the Weibels purchased the historic Stanford Winery in Mission San Jose, which operated from 1869 to 1923. Eventually Weibel moved its operation to Mendocino, where they could expand their vineyards. Reflecting its specialty in sparkling wines, the winery's tasting room is an inverted champagne glass. Inside are soaring beamed ceilings and a bubbling fountain. In addition to a nonalcoholic champagne, they also make a Green Hungarian varietal, which is now nationally known. Visitors are offered ample RV parking, a shaded picnic area adjacent to gardens, and a gift shop.

WHALER VINEYARD
10 miles north of Hopland at 6200 Eastside Rd., Ukiah 95482. Phone & FAX (707) 462-6355. Open for tours daily 10 a.m. to 5 p.m. by appointment.

This small, family owned winery is located on benchland overlooking the Russian River and Ukiah Valley. Annual production is 1800 cases of Zinfandel.

WHITE OAK VINEYARDS
1208 Hayden St., Healdsburg 95448. (707) 433-8429. Open for tasting Fri. through Sun. 10 a.m. to 4 p.m. Tours by appointment only.

Bill Myers moved to Healdsburg from Anchorage, Alaska, where he worked as a salmon fisherman and building contractor. In 1981 he founded White Oak Vineyards in Healdsburg. Today the small, modern facility produces 14,000 cases annually of six varietal wines. Grapes come from estate-owned and contracted vineyards in the Alexander, Dry Creek and Russian River valleys.

WHITEHALL LANE WINERY
1 mile north of Rutherford at 1563 St. Helena Hwy. S. (SR 29), St. Helena 94574. (707) 963-9454. Open for tasting daily 11 a.m. to 6 p.m. Barrel tasting tours by appointment at 1 and 4 p.m.

Whitehall Lane Winery is situated on a 22-acre vineyard at the northern edge of the Rutherford Bench, a geological area regarded as one of the finest locations for growing Cabernet Sauvignon and Merlot. The winery creates small lots of superior Cabernet Sauvignon, Merlot, Chardonnay, Sauvignon Blanc and Riesling.

Z MOORE WINERY
2 miles north of Windsor on US 101 at 3364 River Rd., 95492. (707) 544-3555.

Open for tasting daily 10 a.m. to 5 p.m. 30-minute tours by appointment only.

Housed in a historic hop kiln in the Russian River Valley, Z Moore Winery's name is derived from the combined surnames of the husband-and-wife owners, Daniel and Natalie Zuccarelli-Moore. Since their first vintage in 1985, production has grown to 5000 cases. Mr. Moore's specialty is various dry styles of Gewürztraminer. Also produced is a limited-quantity estate Chardonnay, White Riesling, Petite Sirah, Cabernet Sauvignon and Donato, an old-vine Zinfandel. There are picnic facilities and wine-related gifts available.

ZD WINES

8383 Silverado Tr., Napa 94558. (707) 963-5188. Open for tasting daily 10 a.m. to 4:30 p.m. 40-minute tours by appointment only. $3 tasting fee includes souvenir glass or refund with purchase.

A small family winery, ZD Wines was founded in 1969 and is owned and operated by the de Leuze family. Their philosophy is to produce rich and flavorful wines using a minimum of cellar treatment. In most of its wines, ZD uses the art of blending the same variety of grapes grown in different areas. Their wines were awarded a total of 192 medals in the last 10 years.

ZELLERBACH WINERY

2350 McNab Ranch Rd., Ukiah 95482. (707) 462-2423; FAX (707) 462-9263. Open for tasting and guided tours by appointment 10 a.m. to 5 p.m., Nov. through Feb. from Thur. through Sun., Jun. through Aug. from Mon. through Sun.

Stephen Zellerbach, scion of the Crown Zellerbach paper company, founded the winery in 1982. The label was purchased in 1986 by William Baccala, who relocated the winemaking facility to Mendocino County five years later. Annual production is 130,000 cases of Chardonnay, Merlot, Sauvignon Blanc, White

Zinfandel and Cabernet Sauvignon. Tree-shaded picnic facilities with a view of the valley are available for visitors.

ANNUAL EVENTS

Exact dates, prices and other information about the events listed below may be verified by calling the telephone numbers shown. In addition, some wineries individually sponsor special brunches, dinners and summer concerts; for information on events sponsored by a particular winery, call that winery and ask if a calendar of events is available.

FEBRUARY—

TRI-COUNTY WINE CLASSIC/CITRUS FAIR

Citrus Fairgrounds, Cloverdale. (707) 894-3992. $20 admission includes the fair and one-day wine passport with unlimited tasting of more than 200 award-winning wines. Fair admission only, adults $6, youth $3.

This two-day wine tasting event occurs within a four-day fair, which features a carnival, food, arts and crafts booths, entertainment and live music.

WINTER WINELAND

Various locations, Sonoma County. (707) 433-6782. Admission $15, includes a food and wine tasting ticket good at participating wineries.

Sponsored by the Russian River Wine Road Association, the Alexander, Dry Creek and Russian River Valley's annual three-day celebration of winter include more than 60 wineries, 32 lodges and many restaurants.

MARCH—

HEART OF THE VALLEY BARREL TASTING

Various locations, Kenwood. (707) 833-4666 (St. Francis Winery, Kenwood). Call for admission prices.

Barrel tasting, food sampling, educational

seminars and vineyard tours are part of this two-day event.

ROTARY WINE AUCTION POLENTA FEED
Citrus Fairgrounds, Cloverdale.
(707) 894-3800 (Rotary chairman).
Admission $12.50 including dinner.

A wine auction, lipsynch entertainment and dinner comprise this evening event benefitting C.A.R.E., an educational foundation and community project of the Rotary Club.

RUSSIAN RIVER WINE ROAD BARREL TASTING
Various locations, Sonoma County.
(707) 433-6782. Free admission.

Sponsored by the Russian River Wine Road Association, more than 60 member wineries open for a weekend of barrel tasting. Some wineries offer appetizers and music. Guests can meet the winemakers and taste new releases from the barrel; wine futures are offered at lower prices.

APRIL—

ALL FOOLS DAY RENAISSANCE BANQUET
Chateau de Baun, Fulton.
(707) 571-7500. Admission $50.

The evening's activities include a Medieval-theme costume party, period music, wine and four to six courses of food.

PASSPORT TO DRY CREEK
Dry Creek wineries, Healdsburg.
(707) 433-3031 (Winegrowers of Dry Creek Valley). Admission $30 per day.

Winery and vineyard tours and special events are planned with wine and food pairings at participating wineries over two days.

PICK OF THE VINE
Mayette Center, Santa Rosa.
(707) 433-6782 (Ombudsman Program

of Sonoma County). Admission $20 including a glass and plate for sampling.

Wine tasting and food sampling are this evening's main attractions.

MAY—

BLACK BART FESTIVAL
Downtown Cloverdale.
(707) 894-4470 (Cloverdale Chamber of Commerce). Admission free; call for wine tasting and event prices.

This one-day event features 3K and 10K runs and a dinner dance, along with sheep dog trials, a barbecue, ram auction, model railroad display, square dancing demonstrations, a cow chip toss, wine and beer tasting, a trade show, music and more.

LILLIE LANGTRY DAY
Langtry & Guenoc Estate Vineyards & Winery, Middletown.
(707) 987-2385. Tours on the hour from 10 a.m. to 3 p.m. Free admission.

Tours of the historic Langtry House are offered, and Langtry wines are poured for tasting in this one-day event.

NAPA VALLEY FOOD & WINE SENSATIONAL
Downtown Napa (mailing address: Napa Valley Merchants & Professional Association, 1556 First St., 94559).
(707) 257-0322. Admission free; call for wine tasting prices.

Wine tasting and food sampling are presented with all-day entertainment and an art exhibit.

RUSSIAN RIVER WINE FESTIVAL
Historic Healdsburg Plaza, Healdsburg.
(707) 433-6935, (800) 648-9922 (in California). Advance-purchase tickets $12.50; at the door $15.

This festival features live music, food, arts and crafts, barbecues and formal dinners; 40 Russian River wineries participate in this two-day event.

SPRING MOUNTAIN OPEN HOUSE
Various Spring Mountain wineries, St. Helena.
(707) 963-1616.

The wineries of Spring Mountain are generally closed to the public, but during one weekend some open for wine tasting and conversations with winemakers on style, technique, terrain and grape varieties.

TRAULSEN VINEYARDS OPEN HOUSE
Traulsen Vineyards, Calistoga.
(707) 942-283.

A weekend of activities features roses in full bloom at the winery, along with food, art, wine and music.

WINERY OPEN HOUSE
Vincent Arroyo Winery, Calistoga.
(707) 942-6995; FAX (707) 942-0895.
Admission free.

This two-day open house features wine tasting and light food.

JUNE—

A TASTE OF REDWOOD VALLEY
Various wineries in Redwood Valley and vicinity.
(707) 485-1221 (Gabrielli Winery).
Admission free.

Six wineries participate in a two-day Father's Day celebration of wine tasting and festivities at each location. Special wine discounts are offered.

CLEAR LAKE PERFORMING ARTS CONCERT ON THE LAWN
Langtry House, Guenoc & Langtry Estate Vineyards & Winery, Middletown.
(707) 987-2385.

An afternoon concert is complemented with light food and wine.

NAPA VALLEY WINE AUCTION
Meadowood Resort, St. Helena.
(707) 963-0148.

This charity auction features four days of food and wine tasting; winemaker events, dinners, special tastings and winery open houses.

OX ROAST
Sonoma Plaza, Sonoma.
(707) 938-4626.

This family oriented festival centers around a tri-tip oxburger and ox-dog barbecue at Sonoma Plaza. Wine tasting, art displays, live bands and games for children round out the day.

SONOMA ODYSSEY
Richard's Grove, Santa Rosa.
(707) 433-5349. Call for event prices.

Wine and cookbook authors autograph their works. A huge book sale, wine and food tasting and a jazz concert complete the afternoon's festivities.

SUMMER SOLSTICE CELEBRATION
J. Fritz Winery, Cloverdale.
(707) 894-3389. Admission free.

A day of wine and food pairing is held in the subterranean winery.

WINERY OPEN HOUSE
Dry Creek Vineyard, Healdsburg.
(707) 433-1000, (800) 864-9463.
$7.50 admission fee includes logo glass.

The two-day open house features wine tasting, food sampling and live music.

JULY—

CALIFORNIA WINE TASTING CHAMPIONSHIPS
Greenwood Ridge Vineyards, Philo.
(707) 895-2002. Advance-purchase admission $30 per couple, $45 at the door.

Cheese, wine and chocolate tasting take place with music and picnicking in this two-day event.

OLD-FASHIONED 4TH OF JULY

Sonoma Plaza, Sonoma.
(707) 938-4626 (Sonoma Community
Center). Admission free.

A parade, games, food and wine tasting, and live music comprise this one-day celebration.

SALUTE TO THE ARTS

Sonoma Plaza, Sonoma.
(707) 938-1133 (Summers McCann,
Inc.). Admission free.

A two-day celebration of food, wine and art includes tasting samples provided by Sonoma area restaurants, as well as three stages set for concerts and plays.

SONOMA COUNTY SHOWCASE & WINE AUCTION

Various locations, Sonoma County.
(707) 586-3795; FAX (707) 586-1383
(Sonoma Counties Wineries Association).
Admission and event prices vary.

This event has a different theme each year and features three days of wine tasting, vineyard and winery tours, auctions of old and new vintages and a succession of fine dining experiences.

AUGUST—

MENDOCINO BOUNTY FOOD AND BEVERAGE SHOWCASE

Fetzer Food and Wine Center at
Valley Oaks Farm, Hopland. (mailing
address: Mendocino Bounty, P.O. Box
655, Ukiah, 95482).
(707) 462-3306. Admission $20.

A day-long celebration of the county's diverse agricultural, wine and food businesses includes presentation of the best products of farmers, ranchers, fishermen, vintners, chefs and food artisans.

WINE AND ART FAIR

Chateau St. Jean, Stone Creek Winery
and St. Francis Winery, Kenwood.

(707) 833-4666 (St. Francis Winery).
Call for price information.

This one-day event features wine tasting, food sampling and an exhibit of creations by local artists.

SEPTEMBER—

CLEAR LAKE PERFORMING ARTS WINE AND ART AUCTION

Langtry House, Langtry & Guenoc
Estate Vineyards & Winery, Middletown.
(707) 987-2385. Admission $10.

This one-day event features light food, wine, silent and live auctions, art and live music for the benefit of music scholarships.

FALL FESTIVAL OF LIGHTS

St. Supéry, Rutherford.
(707) 963-4507, (800) 942-0809.
Admission $20 in advance, $25 at
the door.

Wine tasting, Asian-influenced cuisine, a silent auction, drawings and entertainment are featured at this evening benefit for the Solano College Conservatory Theatre.

MENDOCINO COUNTY FAIR & APPLE SHOW

Mendocino County Fair & Apple
Show Fairgrounds, Boonville.
(707) 895-3011. Third Fri. through
Sun of the month, 9 a.m. to noon.
Admission $5; ages 13 to 18, $3; ages 7
to 12, $2.

A three-day fair includes a carnival, food, a vintner's booth, arts and crafts, fresh flowers, a rodeo and sheep dog trials.

STREET CELEBRATION

Downtown Cloverdale.
(707) 894-4470 (Cloverdale Chamber
of Commerce). Admission free; $5 for
three wine tastings.

This day of celebration includes such special events and activities as wine and beer tastings, a frog jumping contest, a pancake breakfast, an antique car show, roller blade competition, sidewalk sales, a mural unveiling, game booths, a swap meet and a farmers market.

OCTOBER—

CRUSH FESTIVAL
Chateau de Baun, Fulton.
(707) 571-7500. Admission to wine-making experience $50; other activities free.

During this Sunday event, visitors have the opportunity for a hands-on wine-making experience. Other events include grape picking, a grape stomp competition, wine judging and a barbecue.

HALLOWEEN MASQUERADE
Chateau de Baun, Fulton.
(707) 571-7500. Admission $30.

An evening masquerade party includes a costume contest sponsored by a local radio station, hors d'oeuvres, wine champagne, dancing and live music.

HARVEST TIME
Various wineries, Healdsburg.
(707) 431-2894 (Alexander Valley Winegrowers). Admission $20.

The afternoon's events include tastings of new releases, library wines, food and wine match-ups at 17 wineries in the Alexander Valley.

KONOCTI WINERY'S HARVEST FESTIVAL
Konocti Winery, Kelseyville.
(707) 279-4395.

This is a two-day event featuring wine specials and tasting, music, a grape stomp, arts and crafts and a farmer's market.

SONOMA COUNTY HARVEST FAIR
Sonoma County Fairgrounds, Santa Rosa.
(707) 545-4203. Fair hours: Fri. 10 a.m. to 8 p.m., Sat. and Sun. to 7 p.m.; tasting Fri. 2 to 7:30 p.m., Sat. and Sun. 12:30 to 5 p.m. Admission $14, ages 7 to 12 $2; tasting fee $6 for three tickets, including glass.

Crafts, artwork, wine tasting and food presentations by local restaurateurs are featured.

ZINFUL CELEBRATION
J. Fritz Winery, Cloverdale.
(707) 894-3389. Free admission.

This weekend celebration has tasting of older vintages and pairings of food and wine.

NOVEMBER—

A TASTE OF HISTORY
Chateau de Baun, Fulton.
(707) 571-7500. Admission $20 including logo glass.

Fifteen wineries of the Russian River Appellation sponsor a library tasting and food pairings as part of this weekend event. A vertical sampling of different vintages is planned.

DECEMBER—

HOLIDAY LIBRARY TASTING
Dry Creek Vineyard, Healdsburg.
(800) 864-9463. Admission $5.

Appetizers, live music, and tasting of library wines are planned for this afternoon event.

Sierra Foothills and the Central Valley

The region of rolling countryside known as the Mother Lode, or the Sierra Foothills, stretches along the western slopes of the Sierra Nevada. The first vineyards here were reputedly planted by miners during the Gold Rush of the mid-1800s. By 1890 there were more than a hundred foothill wineries in operation, but this prosperity was short-lived. As the gold played out the miners moved on, and winemaking dwindled steadily until Prohibition ended it in 1919. Although Prohibition was repealed in 1933, most of the current wineries weren't established in the region until the 1970s. Some of these wineries are housed in the original pre-Prohibition buildings.

Viticulture in the Sierra foothills continues to expand. Although frost danger limits the amount of productive vineyard acreage, the climate is suitable for premium varietals. In fact, the high quality of the grapes has attracted distant wineries like Ridge, Carneros Creek and Sutter Home, which have helped establish the region's reputation for Zinfandel.

Another center of activity is Lodi, where a tenth of the state's wine is produced. Numerous wineries, including several cooperatives, are clustered around the town. From Lodi, the Sacramento Valley extends north nearly 200 miles. This was a thriving wine district prior to Prohibition, but only a few local wineries are now in operation. Detailed information about the Gold Rush towns is contained in the Auto Club of Southern California's *Mother Lode* publication.

Farther south, the Central Valley area, which encompasses the San Joaquin Valley, is California's most productive wine region. Although the wines produced are not of the highest quality due to the extremely warm summer temperatures, the combination of climate and rich soil produce a crop that is nearly double the Napa Valley average per acre. The conditions are particularly good for the production of raisin grapes, as well as table, jug, fortified and dessert wines. The valley produces over half of California's wine grapes; four out of every five bottles is from this area.

Vineyards in the southern part of the San Joaquin Valley are planted largely with raisin and table grapes, such as the Thompson Seedless, but vast vineyards of wine grapes are cultivated near Bakersfield. Farther north, in Modesto, is the largest of California wineries, E. & J. Gallo. The Gallo brothers have used mass production and the valley's high grape yield to full advantage: their numerous vineyards and winemaking facilities (all closed to the public) make them perhaps the largest winery in the world. Recently Gallo turned its attention toward acreage in what is commonly thought of as "wine country"—the northern California coastal region—and has begun phasing out the "Gallo" label. Its labels now include Sheffield, Gallo Livingston Cellars, Wycliffe and Copperidge Chardonnay.

WINERIES OF THE SIERRA FOOTHILLS AND THE CENTRAL VALLEY

A. NONINI WINERY

10 miles northwest of Fresno via McKinley Ave. at 2640 N. Dickenson Ave., 93722. (209) 275-1936. Open for tasting Mon. through Sat. 8 a.m. to 5 p.m. Tours by appointment. Closed noon to 1 p.m. and most major holidays.

This winery has been a family business since its establishment in 1936 by Antonio and Angiolina Nonini. The Nonini wines include four styles of Zinfandel and several generic table wines; these are distributed primarily through local stores and restaurants and sold to the public at the winery.

AMADOR FOOTHILL WINERY

6 miles northeast of Plymouth off Shenandoah Rd. at 12500 Steiner Rd., 95669. (209) 245-6307. Open for tasting Sat. and Sun. noon to 5 p.m. Informal tours upon request.

The winery currently produces about 10,000 cases annually of White and Red Zinfandel, Sangiovese and Sauvignon Blanc; all are made from locally grown grapes. Visitors can see the two-level, energy efficient building which uses a passive rock-bed cooling system. Picnickers are welcome.

ARGONAUT WINERY

5 miles northeast of Ione via SR 124 and Willow Creek Rd.; 13675 Mt. Echo Dr., 95640. (209) 274-4106. Open for tours and tasting by appointment.

A partnership launched this winery in 1976. Primarily a weekend operation, it produces just 2000 cases per year. The emphasis is on varietals, such as estate-grown Barbera and Shenandoah Valley Zinfandel.

BLACK SHEEP VINTNERS

At the west end of Main St. and Murphys Grade Rd. in Murphys (mailing address: P.O. Box 1851, 95247). (209) 728-2157. Open for tasting and tours Sat., Sun. and holidays noon to 5 p.m., Mon. through Fri. by appointment. Closed Thanksgiving and Dec. 25.

Janis and Dave Olson named their winery Black Sheep Vintners because, like a black sheep, they hope to be different. They released their first vintage in 1986 and production is now 3000 cases per year. Their specialty is Zinfandel; also produced are Cabernet Sauvignon and Sauvignon Blanc, all from Sierra foothill grapes.

BOEGER WINERY

½ mile north of US 50 via Schnell School Rd. at 1709 Carson Rd., Placerville 95667. (916) 622-8094. Open for tasting and self-guided tours daily 10 a.m. to 5 p.m.

The Boeger Winery was established in 1973 on a ranch site that dates back to the 1870s. Some of the original stone buildings still stand, including an 1872 wine cellar in which the tasting room is located. Boeger was the first modern-day winery in El Dorado county and now produces 15,000 cases per year from its 55 acres of vineyards. Varietals include Cabernet, Zinfandel, Barbera and Merlot. There is a picnic area for visitors.

CHARLES B. MITCHELL VINEYARDS

3 miles east of Somerset off SR 16 via Fairplay Rd. at 8221 Stoney Creek Rd., 95684. (800) 704-WINE. Open for tasting and tours Wed. through Sun. 11 a.m. to 5 p.m. or by appointment.

This two-acre, oak-shaded winery produces 4000 cases of premium varietals (12 are award winners) such as Chardonnay, Fumé Blanc, Sémillon, Sauvignon Blanc, Chenin Blanc, Johannisberg Riesling, Zinfandel, Cabernet (and Reserve), Meritage,

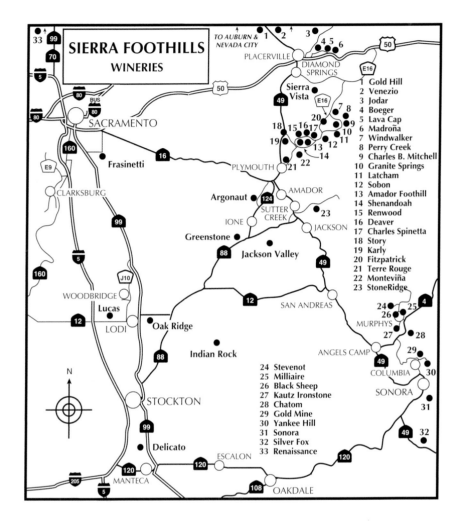

SIERRA FOOTHILLS
WINERIES

TO AUBURN & NEVADA CITY

PLACERVILLE

DIAMOND SPRINGS

Sierra Vista

SACRAMENTO

Frasinetti

CLARKSBURG

PLYMOUTH

AMADOR

Argonaut

SUTTER CREEK

IONE

Greenstone

JACKSON

88

Jackson Valley

WOODBRIDGE

Lucas

LODI

Oak Ridge

Indian Rock

SAN ANDREAS

MURPHYS

ANGELS CAMP

COLUMBIA

SONORA

STOCKTON

Delicato

ESCALON

MANTECA

OAKDALE

1   Gold Hill
2   Venezio
3   Jodar
4   Boeger
5   Lava Cap
6   Madroña
7   Windwalker
8   Perry Creek
9   Charles B. Mitchell
10 Granite Springs
11 Latcham
12 Sobon
13 Amador Foothill
14 Shenandoah
15 Renwood
16 Deaver
17 Charles Spinetta
18 Story
19 Karly
20 Fitzpatrick
21 Terre Rouge
22 Monteviña
23 StoneRidge

24 Stevenot
25 Milliaire
26 Black Sheep
27 Kautz Ironstone
28 Chatom
29 Gold Mine
30 Yankee Hill
31 Sonora
32 Silver Fox
33 Renaissance

N

sparkling wines and Port. There is a historic road dating to the 1850s on the property. A gift shop and picnic facilities are available.

CHARLES SPINETTA WINERY AND WILDLIFE GALLERY

12557 Steiner Rd., Plymouth 95669. (209) 245-3384. Open for tasting Tue. through Sun. 10 a.m. to 4:30 p.m.

This 60-acre facility produces 5000 cases of Zinfandel, Barbera, Chenin Blanc,

Chardonnay, Cabernet and Merlot. A 2500-square-foot wildlife art gallery, custom frame shop, restaurant and picnic facilities are available to visitors.

CHATOM VINEYARDS

8 miles east of Angels Camp at 1969 Douglas Flat, 95229. (209) 736-6500. Open for tasting daily 11 a.m. to 4:30 p.m. Tours by appointment.

Gay Callan's family has been in agriculture for several generations, but her ef-

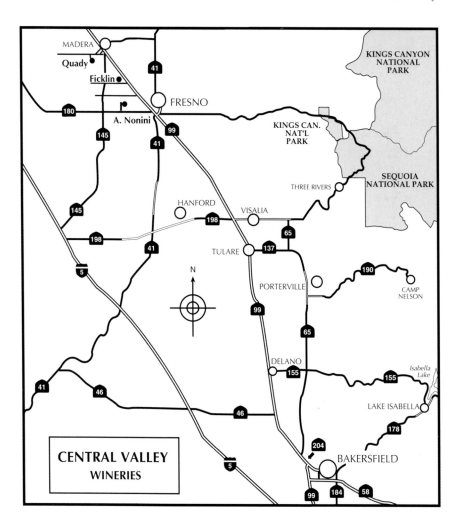

forts began in 1981 when she planted the Esmeralda Valley vineyard and returned to school to study viticulture. Wine production began in 1985 and currently stands at 5000 cases per year of Cabernet Sauvignon, Chardonnay, Sauvignon Blanc, Zinfandel, Merlot and Sémillon.

DEAVER VINEYARDS
12455 Steiner Rd, Plymouth 95669. (219) 245-4099. Open for tasting. Fri. through Mon.

This 200-acre facility produces 1000 cases of Zindandel per year. A lakeside picnic area, refrigerated deli items and a gift shop are available for visitors.

DELICATO VINEYARDS
4 miles north of at Manteca 12001 S. SR 99, 95336. (209) 825-6212, 239-1215. Open for tasting daily 9 a.m. to 5:30 p.m. Tours Fri. at 10 a.m., 2 and 4 p.m., and by appointment.

One of the highlights of September's Delicato Grape Stomp is—the grape stomp. Other events include a classic car show and amateur winemaking.

Glenn Kahl

This facility has been owned and managed by the Indelicato family since the first vineyards were planted in 1924. They now produce 40 million gallons annually of a number of varietal and generic table wines. Each month the winery hosts fund raisers as a community service; the annual Delicato Charity Grape Stomp on Labor Day weekend attracts more than 5000 visitors

DOMAINE DE LA TERRE ROUGE
4 miles northeast of Fiddletown via Shenandoah Rd. at 10801 Dickson Rd., Plymouth (mailing address: P.O. Box 41, 95629). (209) 245-4277. Open for tasting and tours Fri., Sat. and Sun. 11 a.m. to 4 p.m. and by appointment.

Previously Baldinelli Vineyards, the new Terre Rouge winery plans to produce Zinfandel, Riesling and Barbera under the Easton label; additions to the Terre Rouge label will focus on Marsanne, Viognier, Rousanne and a new clone of Syrah. Production is 5000 cases annually. Bill Easton and Jane O'Riordan are the proprietors. A short walk up the hill is rewarded with a pastoral setting and and view of the Sierra Crest; picnic facilities and catered meals for groups are available.

FICKLIN VINEYARDS
30246 Ave. 7.5, Madera 93637. (209) 674-4598. Open for tasting and tours Mon. through Fri. by appointment.

The Ficklin family has been involved in San Joaquin Valley grape-growing since 1911. In the 1940s they planted four Portuguese varietals on an experimental

118

basis, and in 1948 began making port wine from the resulting grapes. The practice has continued to the present day; now the third generation of Ficklins produces nonvintage Tinta Port and special limited bottlings of vintage port.

FITZPATRICK WINERY AND LODGE

7740 Fairplay Rd., Somerset 95684. (916) 620-3248. Open for tasting Sat. and Sun. 11 a.m. to 5 p.m. or by appointment.

Established in 1980, this organic winery produces 3000 cases a year of various wines. A spectacular view exists from the handcrafted, massive log lodge. The winery offers a gift shop, picnic facilities and a bed and breakfast inn. A plowman's lunch is served on Saturday and Sunday.

FRASINETTI WINERY

3 miles east of SR 99 at 7395 Frasinetti Rd., Sacramento (mailing address: P.O. Box 292368, 95829). (916) 383-2444; FAX (916) 383-5825. Open for tasting Tue. through Sat. 11 a.m. to 9 p.m., Sun. to 3 p.m. Closed Jan. 1, Easter, Thanksgiving and Dec. 25.

James Frasinetti, an Italian immigrant, founded his winery in the 1890s, bringing with him "old world" winemaking techniques. The successful winery delivered its wine by horse-drawn wagons and shipped it east by railroad. In 1820, Prohibition prompted the Frasinettis to sell table grapes and produce church wine. In the 1970s, the third generation of Frasinettis began introducing new techniques and equipment. The winery produces varietal wines: Chardonnay, Sauvignon Blanc, Merlot and Cabernet. A restaurant with antique winemaking equipment, gift shop and picnic facilites are on the premises.

GOLD HILL VINEYARD

5660 Vineyard Ln., Placerville 95667. (916) 626-6522. Open for tasting and tours 10 a.m. to 5 p.m. or by appointment.

Nearby the Gold Hill Winery, James Marshall discovered the nugget that started the California Gold Rush, hence the winery's name, and a mile away, one of the earliest California wineries was founded by Robert Chalmers in 1866. Today, 2000 cases a year of Chardonnay, Cabernet Sauvignon, Merlot, Cabernet Franc and white table wine are produced annually on this 35-acre facility. Located in one of the most beautiful settings of the Sierra Nevada foothills, a panoramic view of the American River Valley can be seen from the 1500-square-foot deck, 25 feet above the vineyard. A gift shop and picnic facilities are available for visitors.

GOLD MINE WINERY

¼ mile south of Columbia State Park at 22265 Parrotts Ferry Rd., Sonora 95370. (209) 532-3089. Open for tasting daily 11 a.m. to 5 p.m.

In the heart of California's Mother Lode country, Gold Mine Winery lets its wines age naturally without sophisticated equipment that speeds up that process. Production includes the usual—Chablis, White Zinfandel, Chardonnay, and the unusual—May Wine (with hints of apple and cinammon in the German tradition of Sweet Woodruff), Columbian Gold (sweet red dessert wine flavored with blackcap rasperry and spice), and Spice Jubilee (a blend of spices in a red wine base made to serve hot).

GRANITE SPRINGS WINERY

7 miles southeast of Somerset via Fairplay Rd. at 6060 Granite Springs Rd., 95684. (916) 620-6395; FAX (916) 620-4943. Open for tasting daily 11 a.m. to 5 p.m.

Dug into a granite hillside, Granite Springs was founded by in 1981. The winery is surrounded by vineyards; production of 12,000 cases includes Sauvignon Blanc, Cabernet Sauvignon, Cabernet Franc, Zinfandel, Petite Sirah, vintage Port and Muscat. A picnic area and gift shop are available for visitors. Owners Frank and Patty Latcham also own nearby Latcham Vineyards.

GREENSTONE WINERY

11 miles west of Jackson at jct of SR 88 and Jackson Valley Rd.; 3151 SR 88 (mailing address: P.O. Box 1164, Ione 95640). (209) 274-2238. Open for tasting Wed. through Sun. 10 a.m. to 4 p.m. One-hour tours by appointment.

Greenstone Winery was constructed in 1980 using local greenstone in a French Country design, with a spacious lower level and high sloping ceilings. The height and shape of the building naturally creates different temperature zones for different stages of production and for aging various kinds of wine. The Fowler and Van Spanje families produce a large number of varietal wines. The oak-shaded picnic area overlooks a natural wildlife wetlands and a pond.

INDIAN ROCK VINEYARD

1½ miles southeast of Murphys at 1154 Pennsylvania Gulch Rd. (mailing address: P.O. Box 1526, 95247). (209) 728-2266. Open for tasting Sat., Sun. and holidays 11 a.m. to 5 p.m., or by appointment. Closed Easter, Thanksgiving and Dec 25.

Located at historic Adams Ranch, site of abundant Artesian spring waters, the winery is in a converted, turn-of-the-century dairy. Annual production of Cabernet, Chardonnay, Charbonno and Merlot is about 2000 cases. Visitors are welcome to use the picnic facilities that overlook a trout pond in a serene valley.

JACKSON VALLEY VINEYARDS

1 mile south of Buena Vista at 4851 Buena Vista Rd., Buena Vista/Ione 95640. (209) 274-4721; FAX (209) 274-4723. Open for tasting Wed. through Sun. 11 a.m. to 4 p.m. Tours by appointment. Closed on Jan. 1, Easter, Thanksgiving and Dec. 25.

Founded in 1983, a picturesque duck pond and 60 acres of vines frame the restored century-old barn which houses the Jackson Valley Winery. The 30,000-case annual production is made from estate-grown fruit along with purchased Zinfandel grapes. Premium wines include White Zinfandel, Fleur Blanc, Chardonnay, Cabernet Sauvignon, Zinfandel, Angelica and Port. Picnic facilities and a gift shop are available.

JODAR VINEYARDS & WINERY

2393 Gravel Rd., Placerville 95666. (916) 626-4582. Open for tasting Sat. and Sun. noon to 5 p.m. and by appointment.

Producers of Chardonnay and Cabernet Sauvignon, Jodar is family operated. After 20 years of home winemaking, they decided to make it their living. Searching for two years, they found 40 acres in the Sierra foothills and blasted a vineyard from the granite hillside; the resulting terraces now sweep across the steep slopes. Approximately 3000 cases of wine a year are produced from their eight acres.

KARLY WINERY

4 miles east of SR 49 at 11076 Bell Rd., Plymouth 95669. (209) 245-3922, (800) 654-0880; FAX (209) 245-4874. Open for tasting daily noon to 4 p.m. Tours by appointment.

Buck and Karly Cobb run this small boutique winery, where on weekends oven-fresh sourdough bread is often served in the country-kitchen tasting room. Wines include Zinfandel and White Zinfandel, Sauvignon Blanc, Syrah, Petite Sirah, Mourvédre, Grenache, Chardonnay and Muscat. Production is 10,000 cases a year.

KAUTZ IRONSTONE VINEYARDS

1 mile south of historic Murphy's Hotel at 1894 Six Mile Rd., Murphys 95247. (209) 728-1251; FAX (209) 728-1275.

Open for complimentary wine tasting, cave and winery tours daily 11 a.m. to 5 p.m.

Nestled in the historic Gold Rush town of Murphy's, Kautz Ironstone Vineyards' 1100 acres, once a Wells Fargo station stop, produces Chardonnay, Cabernet Sauvignon, Cabernet Franc, Shiraz, Merlot and Obsession Symphony, as well as Brandy, Apple Brandy and Grappa. Visitors may tour the lavish seven-story facility. The wine caverns were blasted from iron-hard limestone by gold miners, hence the name Ironstone. The caverns maintain a constant 60 degrees, offering guests a cool, heavily-scented walk past aging, wine-filled casks and a waterfall-fed reflection pool. The Music Room features a rotating art exhibit, a collection of antiques and the restored Alhambra Theatre Pipe Organ. The Lakeside Park picnic area is beside a large pond and offers concerts on Sundays in August. Under construction is an outdoor amphitheater. There is a gourmet deli and bakery.

LATCHAM VINEYARDS

1 mile east of Mt. Aukum and SR E16 at 2860 Omo Ranch Rd., Mt. Aukum 95684. (916) 620-6834 or 6642; FAX (916) 620-4943. Open for tasting daily 11 a.m. to 5 p.m.

Located on the north slope of a small, beautiful valley in the Sierra Foothills, Latcham Vineyards was established in 1981. This site was especially chosen for its beauty, fine granitic soil, high elevation and excellent growing conditions: the warm days and cool nights produce an intensity of flavor in the grapes that is not found in other growing areas. Their Zinfandel, White Zinfandel, Cabernet Sauvignon, Cabernet Franc, Petite Sirah, Port, Merlot, Chardonnay and Sauvignon Blanc have all won critical acclaim. There are picnic tables, a spacious parking area and a gift shop for visitors.

LAVA CAP WINERY

3 miles north of Placerville in the center of Apple Hill, at 2221 Fruitridge Rd., Placerville 95667. (916) 621-0175. Open for tasting and tours daily 11 a.m. to 5 p.m. Closed major holidays.

The name "Lava Cap" emphasizes the special soil of the vineyards, dating back more than 10 million years to the period when volcanic ash and lava covered the western Sierras; the owners believe that this special soil imparts intense flavors and aromas to their wines. The 49ers of the Gold Rush realized that the best gold-bearing streams were buried under a lava cap of thick volcanic ash; since then, erosion has removed most of the lava cap. Annual production of 10,000 cases includes Cabernet Blanc and Sauvignon, Chardonnay, Fumé Blanc, Merlot, Muscat Canelli, White Zinfandel and Zinfandel.

THE LUCAS WINERY

2 miles west of Lodi off Turner Rd. at 18196 N. Davis Rd., 95242. (209) 368-2006. Barrel tasting and tours by appointment only.

David Lucas produces 1000 cases a year of Zinfandel from five acres of low-yielding, 65-year-old vines. The barrel aging, storage and tasting rooms are housed in three compact buildings adjacent to his home on a country road near Lodi. Tours provide a thorough look at a small-scale, labor-intensive, family winemaking operation.

MADROÑA VINEYARDS

5 miles east of Placerville on US 50, exit left on Carson Rd., right on High Hill Rd. to the end (mailing address: P.O. Box 454, Camino 95709). (916) 644-5948. Open for tasting daily 11 a.m. to 5 p.m. Tours by appointment.

The vineyards at Madroña—perhaps California's highest at an elevation of 3000 feet—were planted in 1973-74, and initially the yields were sold to other wineries. In 1980 the winery was constructed, and Madroña produces Johannisberg Riesling, Gewürztraminer, Merlot, Cabernet Franc and late-harvest dessert wines, among others.

MILLIAIRE WINERY
276 Main St., Murphys (mailing address: P.O. Box 1554, 95247). (209) 728-1658. Open for tasting and tours daily 11 a.m. to 4:30 p.m.

Steve Millier began his winemaking career in 1975 at the David Bruce Winery in Santa Cruz. In 1982, he and his wife Elizabeth left the California coast for the Sierra Nevada mountains and moved to Murphys, where Steve worked as winemaker at Stevenot Winery until 1989. In 1983, the Milliers founded their winery ("milliaire" means "milestone" in French), which produces 2000 cases per year of Cabernet Sauvignon, Chardonnay, Merlot, Gewürztraminer, Sauvignon Blanc, Zinfandel and several dessert wines, all from Sierra foothills fruit.

MONTEVIÑA
3 miles northeast of Plymouth at 20680 Shenandoah School Rd. (mailing address: P.O. Box 100, 95669). (209) 245-6942. Open for tasting daily 11 a.m. to 4 p.m.

Monteviña is Amador County's first post-Prohibition winery and also the largest. Production is currently 80,000 to 100,000 cases annually of Zinfandel, White Zinfandel, Sangiovese, Barbera, Aleatico, Brioso, Cabernet Sauvignon, Chardonnay and Fumé Blanc. A gift shop and tree-shaded picnic area are available to visitors.

NEVADA CITY WINERY
321 Spring St., Nevada City, 95959. (916) 265-9463. Open for tasting daily noon to 5 p.m. $5 per person, minimum $40 fee for group tours by appointment.

An old tin garage in picturesque Nevada City houses this three-level winery

founded in 1980. Grapes purchased from Nevada County vineyards account for an annual 8000-case output of varietal and generic wines. Visitors are able to observe the production area from the tasting room.

OAK RIDGE VINEYARDS
1 mile east of Lodi at 6100 E. Hwy. 12, 95240. (209) 369-4758. Open for tasting daily 9 a.m. to 5 p.m. Tours offered during the fall crush season by appointment.

Oak Ridge is one of several wineries in the Lodi region owned by a growers' cooperative. Owned and operated by many of the same grower families that founded the winery over six decades ago in 1934, it has developed a full line of table, dessert and aperitif wines. Visitors are offered a variety of samples in the tasting room/gift shop, which is housed in a converted 50,000 gallon redwood aging tank. Tables are available for picnickers.

PERRY CREEK VINEYARDS
16 miles south of Placerville via Mt. Aukum Rd. at 7400 Perry Creek Rd. (mailing address P.O. Box 304, Somerset 95684). (916) 620-5175, (800) 880-4026. Open for tasting and tours Sat. and Sun. 11 a.m. to 5 p.m. and by appointment.

Michael Chazen made his fortune in the textile industry but grew tired of the international commute that had him spending half his time in the United States and half in Korea. He and his wife, Alice, now run this state-of-the-art oasis near the middle fork of the Consumnes River. Winemaker Nancy Steel vinifies Perry Creek's wines— including a dry Alsatian-style Riesling and a White Zinfandel "for people who don't like White Zinfandel." Fifty acres of vineyards are planted to Nebbiolo, Sangiovese, Muscat Canelli, Syrah, Viognier, Zinfandel, Merlot and Cabernet Franc. Production is 6000 cases per year. There are picnic facilities, a gourmet gift shop and a display of Chazen's collection of classic automobiles.

QUADY
13181 Rd. 24, Madera 93637. (209) 673-8068, (800) 733-8068. Open for tasting and tours Mon. through Fri. 9 a.m. to 5 p.m.; Sat. and Sun. by appointment.

Andrew Quady began making vintage port from Amador County Zinfandel grapes in 1975. His original compact winery building forms one wing of the modern concrete and stucco facility which opened in 1985. Quady produces about 20,000 cases per year of premium dessert wines. The equipment includes stainless steel fermentors, an ancient crusher and French oak barrels. His wine creations include Orange-Muscat "Essencia" and Black Muscat "Elysium."

RENAISSANCE VINEYARD & WINERY
12585 Rices Crossing Rd., Oregon House (mailing address: P.O. Box 1000, 95962). (916) 692-2222. Open for tasting Wed. through Sun. $5 fee for 2½-hour guided tours by appointment at 1 p.m.

Reniassance is a 1400-acre, forested mountain retreat on the western slopes of the Sierra Nevada, with picturesque terraced vineyards and a majestic, three-level, round sparkling white building. Owned by Fellowship of Friends, an international interdenominational organization committed to the arts, it has a 300-seat auditorium and a fine arts museum filled with Ming Dynasty furniture. The 365-acre estate was originally a place for members to gather and take classes in the arts, philosophies and languages, but it was decided to go commercial with a winery. Production is 10,000 cases of quality Cabernet Sauvignon, Chardonnay, Sauvignon Blanc, Riesling, Dry White Riesling and

late harvest wines. The winery offers a restaurant and gift shop for visitors.

RENWOOD WINERY INC.
3 miles northeast of Plymouth via Shenandoah Rd. at 12225 Steiner Rd., 95669. (209) 245-6979. Open for tasting daily 11 a.m. to 4:30 p.m. Tours by appointment. Closed major holidays.

The 30,000-case winery features Grandpère, America's oldest 125-year-old Zinfandel vineyard. Renwood produces many world-class wines, including Barbera, Syrah, Fiddletown Zinfandel, Sangiovese and Viognier. Santino wines include White Zinfandel and Muscato del Diavolo. Winemaker Scott Harvey's German background has taught him how to make the unusual Zinfandel and Amador Ice wines. Picnic facilities are available. The tasting room has a selection of refrigerated deli items and there is a gift shop.

SHENANDOAH VINEYARDS
5 miles northeast of Plymouth via Shenandoah Rd. at 12300 Steiner Rd., 95669. (209) 245-4455. Open for tasting and tours daily 10 a.m. to 5 p.m.

Leon Sobon left his job as a research scientist to launch his own winery in 1977. With the help of his wife Shirley and six children, he produces about 30,000 cases each year. Forty-two acres of vineyard adjoin the hilltop winery; all are farmed organically. The wine list includes four dry varietals, along with three dessert wines.

SIERRA VISTA WINERY
12 miles southeast of Placerville via Pleasant Valley Rd. and Leisure Ln. at 4560 Cabernet Wy., 95667. (916) 622-7221. Open for tasting daily 11 a.m. to 4 p.m. or by appointment.

John and Barbara MacCready founded their small winery in 1977. The label takes inspiration from their 270-degree view of the Coast Range and the

Sierras. In addition to Cabernet Sauvignon, Chardonnay, Fumé Blanc and Zinfandel, attention is also focused on Syrah, Viognier, Grenache, Mourvèdre, Cinssault and other varieties of the Rhône region of France. Annual production now stands at 8000 cases. Shaded picnic areas provide a great view of the Sierras.

SILVER FOX VINEYARDS

4683 Morningstar Ln., Mariposa 95338. (209) 966-4800; FAX (209) 966-4369. Open for tasting and tours Sat., from Jun. through Aug. noon to 4:30 p.m., and by appointment.

Established in 1989 by Marvin and Karen Silver and Joe and Ingrid Fox, the winery produces premium hand-crafted wines made from from 7½ acres of vineyards. The winery has several gold medal-winning wines; it produces 1000 cases annually of Cabernet Sauvignon, Merlot and Zinfandel. Picnic facilities are available.

SOBON ESTATE

7 miles northeast of Plymouth at 14430 Shenandoah Rd., 95669. (209) 245-6554. Open for tasting and tours daily 10 a.m. to 5 p.m.

Leon and Shirley Sobon celebrated their 30th wedding anniversary by opening this new winery near their Shenandoah Vineyards—Sobon Estate. Formerly the D'Agostini Winery, this historical landmark is the third-oldest winery in the state, built by Adam Uhlinger in 1856. The 60 acres of adjoining vineyard are planted to Zinfandel and Sangiovese. The original cellars are still in use, and staves from six of the old redwood tanks panel the tasting room, which is housed in what was once D'Agostini's warehouse and bottling room. Early winemaking and agricultural equipment is on display in the Shenandoah Valley Museum across from the tasting room. A picnic area fronts the winery.

SONORA WINERY AND PORT WORKS

4 miles southwest of Sonora via Old Wards Ferry Rd. at 17500 Route 5 Rd. (mailing address: P.O. Box 242, 95370). (209) 532-PORT. Open for tasting and tours by appointment and selected weekends.

Established in 1986, the winery's mission is to produce world class Port-style and Red Zinfandel wines. Yearly production of 2500 cases includes award-winning Port from Portugese varieties, Savignon Blanc and Zinfandel.

STEVENOT WINERY

3 miles north of Murphys at 2690 San Domingo Rd., 95247. (209) 728-3436. Open for tasting daily 10 a.m. to 5 p.m. Tours by appointment.

Stevenot is one of the most prominent family names in Mother Lode country. Owner Barden Stevenot founded the winery in 1974 on the site of the former Shaw Ranch, and many of the winery buildings date back to the turn of the century. In a restored hay barn and in a newer, similarly styled structure, 45,000 cases of wine per year are produced. Twenty-seven acres of vineyards are planted to Cabernet Sauvignon, Chardonnay, Merlot and Zinfandel. The winery also makes a dessert wine, available only at the winery. Refrigerated deli items are sold in the rustic tasting room and gift shop, built in 1903, and picnic tables are shaded by grape arbors in a garden setting.

STONERIDGE

4 miles southeast of Sutter Creek at 13862 Ridge Rd. E., 95685. (209) 223-1761. Open for tasting and tours by appointment.

StoneRidge is one of the smallest commercial wineries in the foothill region, producing less than 1500 gallons a year. Owners Gary and Loretta Porteous do all the work themselves, from pruning to bottling. Visitors are also welcome to

taste the two StoneRidge wines:
Zinfandel and Ruby Cabernet.

STORY WINERY
10525 Bell Rd., Plymouth 95669. (209) 245-6208. Open for tasting and tours Mon. through Fri. noon to 4 p.m., Sat. and Sun. 11 a.m. to 5 p.m.

Established in 1973, Story produces 5000 cases annually of Zinfandel, Mission and Chenin Blanc. Picnic facilities and a gift shop are available.

VENEZIO VINEYARDS
3520 Overton Rd., Cool 95614. (916) 885-6815; FAX (916) 885-6815. Open for tasting by appointment.

This microwinery, the smallest in El Dorado County, produces 700 cases each year from a 1½-acre vineyard. Wines produced are Cabernet, Zinfandel, Chardonnay and Sauvignon Blanc.

WINDWALKER VINEYARD
7360 Perry Creek Rd., Somerset 95684. (916) 620-4054. Open for tasting Sat. and Sun. 11 a.m. to 5 p.m. or by appointment.

This eight-acre winery was established in 1986 and produces 3000 cases annually of Chardonnay, Chenin Blanc, Cabernet Sauvignon, Zinfandel, Johannisberg Riesling, and red and white table wines. A gift shop and picnic facilities are available for visitors.

YANKEE HILL WINERY
¾ mile east of Columbia on Yankee Hill Rd. (mailing address: P.O. Box 330, 95310). (209) 533-2417. Open for tasting daily 10 a.m. to 5 p.m. Tours upon request.

Built in 1970, Yankee Hill Winery produces an assortment of table, sparkling and berry wines. These currently total 2500 cases a year. Vineyards are being planted, and in the meantime grapes are purchased locally. The winery has a deck area with tables and a shaded picnic area.

ANNUAL EVENTS

Exact dates, prices and other information about the events listed below may be verified by calling the telephone numbers shown. In addition, some wineries individually sponsor special brunches, dinners and summer concerts; for information on events sponsored by a particular winery, call that winery and ask if a calendar of events is available.

MARCH/APRIL—

EL DORADO COUNTY PASSPORT WEEKEND
Various wineries and locations, El Dorado County (mailing address: El Dorado Winery Association, P.O. Box 1614, Placerville 95667). (916) 622-7221. Admission $30 per weekend.

A two-weekend event of wine tasting includes library vintages, new releases, wine from the barrel, wine and food pairing, demonstrations, vineyard tours and music.

LODI SPRING WINE SHOW AND FOOD FAIRE
Lodi Grape Festival Grounds, 413 E. Lockeford St., Lodi 95240. (209) 369-2771. Call for ticket prices.

Forty wineries and 10 restaurants provide samples of wine and food. The two-day event also offers fine arts, photography, craft displays and cooking demonstrations.

MAY—

A DAY OF WINE AND ROSES IN THE MOTHER LODE
Sierra Vista Winery, Placerville. (916) 622-7221; Rosarian Muriel Humenick of Rose Acres, (916) 626-1722; Jan Condit of the Fleming Jones Homestead, (916) 626-9545. Admission $2-3 for tasting and commemorative

rose glass; tours free; optional lunch prices vary.

Informal Heritage Rose Garden and winery tours are the focus of this day's event; visitors may join the tour at any point. Lunches need to be reserved in advance with Zachary Jacques Restaurant and are delivered to Sierra Vista Winery, or visitors may picnic on their own.

MEMORIAL WEEKEND
Sierra Vista Winery, Placerville. (916) 622-7221. Admission free.

Rhône tasting and Special Reserve wines are poured and appetizers are served over two days.

MOTHER'S DAY AT SIERRA VISTA WINERY
Sierra Vista Winery, Placerville. (916) 622-7221. Admission free.

Rhône tasting and hors d'oeuvres are featured in this day's events.

SIERRA SHOWCASE OF WINE
Amador County Fairgrounds, Plymouth. (209) 267-5978 (The Ark of Amador and Calaveras). Call for ticket prices; order in advance or purchase at the gate.

The day's activities include a barbecue, wine, fruit and cheese tasting, art show, live music and an auction.

WINERY OPEN HOUSE
Madroña Vineyards, Camino. (916) 644-5948. Admission free.

This two-day open house features wine tasting.

JUNE—

THE BIG EASY AT STEVENOT
Stevenot Winery, Murphys. (209) 728-3436. Admission free; nominal fees for food samples and wine.

Ten restaurant teams from Northern California who carry Stevenot wine

participate in a day-long Cajun cookoff and sell samples of favorite Cajun recipes.

BIG TWO WEEKEND
Sierra Vista Winery, Placerville. (916) 622-7221. Admission free.

The winery pours new releases of barrel fermented Chardonnay, Cabernet Sauvignon and Five Star Reserve Cabernets in this two-day event.

FAIRPLAY WINE FESTIVAL
At seven wineries in the Fairplay area, Somerset. (916) 620-5175 (Perry Creek Vineyards). Admission free; nominal fees for food samples.

A variety of live music, wine tasting, cheeses, gourmet foods, art and craft exhibits, games and special wine discounts take place over two days.

ZINFANDEL WEEKEND
Sierra Vista Winery, Placerville. (916) 622-7221. Admission free.

Older Zinfandels from the Sierra Vista Winery cellar, new releases and their Five Star Reserve are featured in this event which coincides with the official two-day Sierra Foothill Weekend.

JULY—

MUSIC AT THE WINERIES ARTS FESTIVALS
Various wineries, Amador County. (209) 267-0211 (Arts Council). Admission $20 for 3 events including wine tasting and food; call for discount information.

Theater and live music, hors d'ouevres and wine tasting are the day's features.

SEPTEMBER—

BLUEGRASS CONCERT
Stevenot Winery, Murphys. (209) 728-3436. Admission $12.50 for 1 glass of wine and appetizers.

Bluegrass music, wine tasting, and appetizers are featured on this one-day event benefitting the Calaveras County Women's Crisis Center.

DELICATO GRAPE STOMP
Delicato Vineyards, Lodi.
(209) 825-6213. Admission $4 for ages 14 and up.

This one-day event includes a grape stomp, a car show, amateur wine-making, live music, and arts and crafts displays.

OCTOBER—

GOLD RUSH DAY AND CALAVERAS GRAPE STOMP
Murphys Park, Murphys.
(209) 795-3850. Call for ticket prices.

This annual charity event includes a grape stomp competition every half hour, live entertainment, food, a dunk tank, face painting and wine tasting from all seven Calaveras wineries; there is also a Gold Rush Street Faire and Run.

WINE APPRECIATION WEEK
Various wineries and locations, Amador County.

(209) 245-6208; FAX (209) 245-6619, Story Winery. Admission free.

Live music, barrel and new release tasting, barbecues, food and meet-the-winemaker events take place over two days.

NOVEMBER—

A FAIRPLAY HOLIDAY
Seven wineries in the Fairplay area, Somerset.
(916) 620-5175 (Perry Creek Vineyards). Admission free.

For five days each week through Christmas, wines are discounted and weekly tastings highlight different varietals; also available are harvest-table foods, gift purchases and educational information.

FALL VERTICAL TASTINGS
Sierra Vista Winery, Placerville.
(916) 622-7221. Admission $10 for 8 tastings; reservations required.

Vertical tastings with food are held over two weekends.

127

Glossary of Wine Terms

Acidity—
a term used in wine tasting to indicate agreeable sharpness or tartness produced by natural fruit acids; a good wine should have balanced acidity and sweetness.

Aging—
a winemaking process that involves storage of wine, most often in oak barrels of various origins, redwood casks or stainless steel tanks, and in the bottle. During aging, the wine breathes through the container ("cooperage"), and it takes on certain characteristics of the container (an "oakey" taste from the oak barrels).

Agrafe—
a metal clip used to secure the cork during secondary champagne fermentation.

Alcohol—
shown on the label in a percentage factor; alcohol preserves wine and is actually ethanol.

Aldehyde—
formed during oxidation at the stage between alcohol and acid; removed by adding sulfur dioxide.

Alembic—
a pot-type still normally used in making brandy.

Allelopathic cover crop—
a plant with natural weed-suppressing tendencies.

Anthocyanins—
matter under the outer layer of the grape's skin that has color.

Appellation—
the designation of a wine's geographic origin, such as the name of a particular vineyard, county or district.

Aroma—
the scent that emanates from wine, having to do with the grape it is made from.

Astringency—
the mouth-puckering sensation produced by tannin in wine; young wines with high astringency usually smooth out with age.

Back blend—
the process of adding unfermented grape juice to fermented wine or unoaked wine to barrel-fermented wine.

Balance—
a harmonious expression of several elements in a wine.

Barbera grape—
a red vinifera variety that is grown on more than 15,000 acres of the central

valley in California, as well as in Argentina and Brazil. It originates from the Piedmont region of Italy.

Barrel fermentation—
oak-barrel fermentation which adds oak character to wine.

Barrique—
a standard size of wooden barrel, 225 liters (60 gallons U.S.), holding approximately 24 cases. (Also see "puncheons").

Benchland—
a flat terrain between two slopes.

Bentonite—
a fining agent consisting of volcanic ash in a fine clay form.

Big—
a term for describing wine that has a full, tannic flavor, with a high content of alcohol and glycerine.

Blind tasting—
tasting of wines that are purposely unknown to the taster.

Blush wine—
a light rosé wine, ranging in color from pink to peach.

Body—
the consistency or "weight" of wine on the tongue. Red wines tend to be heavy-bodied and white wines lighter.

Bottle-fermented—
a champagne process whereby the second fermentation occurs in the bottle.

Botrytis cinerea—
called "noble rot," Botrytis is a unique plant mold producing concentrated sweetness and flavor in affected grapes; it plays a significant part in the production of sweet white wines in Europe and in California's coastal counties.

Bottle sickness—
a temporary decline in a wine's quality that results from agitation during bottling or shipping; the wine normally recovers within a few weeks.

Bouquet—
the fragrance of a wine created by fermentation and aging, developing as the wine matures (different from "aroma").

Brettanomyces—
a yeast which reacts to a wine's amino acids, resulting in an unpleasant, "mousey" aroma and taste.

Brix—
a measurement multiplied by .55 to obtain a wine's probable alcohol content. Brix measure determines soluble solids (sugar) content in grapes.

Brut—
a term used to describe extremely dry champagnes (containing usually less than 1.5 percent alcohol).

Cabernet Sauvignon grapes—
used for the majority of reds in California, this variety grows best in the warmer vineyards across America and also in Chile.

Carbonic Maceration—
a technique of fermentation employed in the production of Beaujolais-style wines in which whole grape clusters and their stems are fermented together; the grapes are usually pressed afterward to extract the wine, which is light, fruity and intended for early consumption.

Cassis—
a black-currant flavor which may be detected in wine.

Cellar—
a storage area where wines are aged. It also describes the action taken to age a wine, namely "cellaring a wine."

Character—
Appearance, scent and taste of a particular wine that distinguishes it from others.

Chardonnay grape—
the most used white variety over the last two decades from Canada to South America. It varies from dry to sweet and can be rich or lean, depending upon winemaking style.

Charmat (or bulk) process—
the method of producing sparkling wines in which the second fermentation is conducted in large glass-lined tanks, thereby speeding up production and lowering cost.

Chenin Blanc grape—
a white variety grown in over 29,000 acres of the central valley in California, used mostly for blends in sparkling wine. It is also used for sweet wines in France.

Clarification—
removal of sediment from aged wines before bottling by racking, fining or filtering.

Clone—
an asexually propagated, genetically-identical vine cloned from a single source.

Cold fermentation—
a process that ferments white must at a lower temperature, producing a lighter, crisper wine.

Complexity—
the balance of a wine's features such as aroma, bouquet, texture and flavor, as well as the winemaking process.

Cooperage—
the general term used for bulk containers in which wine is aged, particularly wooden barrels and tanks.

Crush—
the processing of grapes at harvest, involving crushing them to release the juices. "Harvest" and "crush" are sometimes used interchangeably.

Cuvée—
a blend of wines bottled as one lot; usually refers to the blend of still wines used to make champagnes.

Decant—
to pour wine from the bottle into a serving container so that sediment remains in the bottle and clear wine is obtained.

Demi-sec—
a sparkling wine that is somewhat dry to sweet, with more than 2 percent residual sugar.

Dessert wine—
wines such a Port, Sherry, Madeira, Muscatel or Tokay, that have an alcohol content of 17 to 24 percent alcohol; this is usually achieved by adding spirits or brandy.

Disgorge—
to remove sediment from sparkling wines by uncorking the bottle and allowing the frozen plug in the neck (where solids have settled during riddling) to escape.

Dosage—
the small amount of syrup and aged wine added to sparkling wines after disgorging; the dosage determines the sweetness of champagnes.

Downey mildew—
a vine fungus on the bottom of the leaves that looks like white mildew.

Drip irrigation—
at its most modern, a calibrated system of pipes that deliver water to the vineyard.

Dry—
the majority of red wines, and some white wines, are dry, with less than 0.5 percent of residual sugar.

Dry farming—
without using irrigation, cultivation is achieved by using mulch around the vines to protect natural moisture.

Enology (oenology)—
the science of wine and winemaking.

Estate bottled—
wine that is fermented, aged and bottled by a winery located in the viticultural area named on the wine's label, and made from grapes grown in that area by the winery.

Fermentation—
the process of sugar being converted by yeast enzymes to alcohol and carbon dioxide, thereby transforming grape juice to wine.

Filtration—
the process of wine clarification by pouring through porous substances.

Fining—
the method of wine clarification which uses a settling agent such as egg white or gelatin, which takes particles with it as it settles.

Finish—
a wine-tasting term referring to palate sensation after the wine is swallowed, preceding the aftertaste.

Flor—
a yeast growth which develops on the surface of wines in partially filled containers, giving flor sherries their distinctive flavor.

Fortified—
the addition of high-alcohol spirit to wine.

Free-run juice—
juice that drains from grapes during crushing before the skins are squeezed in a press.

French Colombard grape—
covering about 73,000 acres in California, mostly in the central valley, this is the most popular grape for white still and sparkling wines.

Generic—
a term applied to wines that are named after European wine-producing districts (e.g., Burgundy, Chablis, Sauterne), these also include those bearing general labels (e.g., claret, chianti, vin rosé). Usually several grape varieties are blended to make generic wines, which are generally less expensive than varietal wines.

Gewürztraminer grape—
a white grape with pink skin that is grown on more than 4000 acres in California. It is also known as Traminer or Red Traminer. It is most known in France's Alsace region.

Gondola—
an open trailer that transports grapes from field to crush.

Graft—
A vine grafted to disease-resistant rootstock.

Green Hungarian grape—
a white vinifera that is grown on about 500 acres in California.

Handmade wines—
some small wineries use this process, which requires much manual labor and attention.

Hydroponic viticulture—
the process of using gravel or other soil-free substance to cultivate vines by filtering water with inorganic nutrients through it.

Imperial—
a larger bottle equal to eight standard bottles.

Jeroboam—
a larger bottle equalling six standard bottles.

Jug wine—
low-quality wines sold in large containers for a low price.

Late harvest—
a term used to describe a wine (frequently Riesling) made from grapes picked at an advanced state of ripeness, giving the wine extra sweetness and flavor from which dessert wines can be made.

Lees—
the leftover sediment in a cask after the racking of the wine.

Legs—
the pattern produced when wine is swirled in a glass, clinging to the sides as it descends.

Length—
An evaluation term referring to the amount of time the taste of a wine lasts after swallowing.

Magnum—
a bottle size double the standard, as in "a magnum of champagne."

Malolactic fermentation—
a natural secondary process of fermentation that results in a less tannic, subtler taste. The malic acid converts to lactic acid and carbon dioxide, releasing unpleasant-smelling gases as it does so.

Merlot grape—
acreage planted to Merlot increases every year; it is the grape most in favor. This honey-flavored red grape is blended into Bordeaux and also some varietals.

Méthode champenoise—
the original French method of producing champagnes, in which the wine undergoes its second fermentation in the bottle; this process is costlier and more time-consuming than the Charmat process. Sparkling wines produced by the *champenoise* method may bear the label "naturally fermented in *this* bottle."

Methoxypyrazines—
substances that display an herbaceous flavor in wines such as Cabernet Sauvignon and Sauvignon Blanc prior to ripeness.

Microclimate—
a small geographical area with its own variant climate and topography, affecting the soil and growing conditions.

Muscat Blanc grape—
a white grape that is planted on more than 1500 acres in California. It is referred to as a "great European Muscat" variety and is used for dry and sweet wines. In Argentina and Chile it is called the Moscatel.

Must—
the mixture of grape juice, pulp and skin produced by crushing.

Natur (or Natural)—
a term used to describe the driest champagnes, to which no dosage has been added.

Nebbiolo grape—
a red grape from Northern Italy where it is used for Barolo. Also grown in Argentina and Uruguay, it is minimally grown in California but acreage is increasing.

Nematodes—
a parasite (microscopic worm) that infects the roots of vines, but without the deadly effect of phylloxera.

Nonvintage—
a term referring to wine bottles that aren't identified by a vintage year on the label; nonvintage wines often contain a blend of grapes from different years.

Nose—
a general term referring to the combined grape aroma and bouquet of a wine.

Open-lyre trellis—
a more expensive cultivation trellis of two diagonally placed posts supporting dual canopies from one vine.

Organic viticulture—
grapes grown and wine produced without the use of synthetic pesticides, fertilizers or other synthetic chemicals.

Oxidized—
the word used to describe wine that has had excessive exposure to air, damaging the flavor and color. Oxidation results from improper handling or storage.

pH—
a chemical measurement of acidity. Acidity affects the resulting wine in all aspects.

Petite Sirah grape—
a red, spicy grape planted in California's central valley; more than 6000 acres are used to produce over 70 varietals.

Phylloxera vastatrix—
a plant louse that attacks the roots of grapevines. Phylloxera was responsible for the massive destruction of European vineyards in the late 19th century; a remedy, grafting European vines (*Vitis vinifera*) to American rootstock (*Vitis labrusca*), was discovered in time to halt the destruction of California vineyards. A new type of louse, to which currently planted rootstock is not resistant, now threatens thousands of acres of California vineyards.

Pigeage—
now refers to most manual mixing of red musts, but was originally the foot-crushing of grapes.

Pinot Blanc grape—
about 2000 acres of this white grape are planted within California; it is also grown in Argentina and Brazil.

Pinot Noir grape—
a red grape grown in cooler areas of California, Oregon and South America, and most used for Burgundy-style red wines.

Pomace—
grape skins, seeds and pulp that remain after the grapes have been crushed and the wine pressed or drawn off.

Press—
a basic piece of winemaking equipment, used to crush grapes to obtain the grape juice.

Private reserve—
usually used to denote a particular winery's aged, specially made wine.

Prohibition—
the 18th Amendment to the United States Constitution of 1920 which forbade "the manufacture, sale or transport of intoxicating liquors"; it was repealed in 1933.

Pruning—
the cutting back of vines during winter.

Pumping over—
a part of the fermentation process in which red wine is pumped from the bottom of the tank to the top; this also aids in color evenness.

Puncheons—
barrels that are four times the standard barrique size.

Racking—
a method of wine clarification in which clear wine is drawn from one container to another, leaving behind a deposit of sediment (lees).

Refractometer—
the instrument used to measure degrees of Brix, or the level of sugar in grapes.

Residual sugar—
the unfermented sugar left in a wine; usually indicated on the wine label.

Riddling—
the process of collecting sediment in the necks of champagne bottles by placing the bottles upside-down in a special rack, and turning them daily to work the deposit into the necks.

Rootstock—
the grapevine roots and stem that are chosen for suitability to soil and resistance to disease, as well as compatibility with the grapes to be grafted. Also refers to the roots of a grafted vine, usually phylloxera-resistant.

Sake—
Japan's national rice wine. Over the centuries, brewmasters have improved sake-making techniques, and today they have a fruity, nutty flavor with a smooth aftertaste. The process has two steps: conversion of starch to sugar, and fermentation into alcohol. Sake's alcohol content is between 16 and 18 percent, slightly higher than grape wine, but containing no sulfites or preservatives.

Scion—
the grafted vine belonging to the producer rather than the rootstock.

Sec—
a term used to describe still or sparkling wines that are semi-dry; literally, "dry" in French.

Sediment—
the deposit of particles that have settled in the cask or bottle during aging.

Sémillon grape—
a popular white grape planted on more than 4000 acres of California's vineyards, used primarily in dry and sweet white Bordeaux.

Skin contact—
grape skins in contact with grape juice prior to pressing, which affects tannins and wine color.

Smudge pots—
small fuel burners set out in the vineyard to protect from frost.

Sparkling wine—
effervescent wine made by a second fermentation in the bottle or in a pressurized container.

Sweet wine—
wine with a residual sugar of 1 percent or more, although sweetness can be noticeable at 0.5 to 0.7 percent.

Solera—
a tier of casks used to blend sherries of different ages by drawing the oldest wine from the bottom cask for bottling and replacing it with newer wine from the casks above.

Sulfur dioxide—
added to wine as a bactericide and preservative.

Sur lees—
wine kept on the lees instead of being racked or filtered prior to bottling.

Syrah grape—
a red grape originating in the Northern Rhône region; although previously rare in California, it is increasingly being used here and in Argentina.

Tannin—
an acid contained in grape skins and seeds which is released during crushing and fermentation; it gives wine astringency. Because they are fermented in contact with the grape skins, red wines have a higher tannin content than white wines and are bitter when young, but it is necessary for the aging of red wines.

Tartrates—
clear, harmless crystals of tartaric acid that form as wine is aged; their presence is particularly common in white wine.

Terroir—
the total growing environment that affects vine life.

Thompson Seedless grape—
a basic table wine white grape, mostly grown in California's central valley and in Chile.

Topped—
addition of wine into casks to ensure that there is no air at the top.

Transfer method—
a variation of the *champenoise* method of producing sparkling wine; the wine is fermented in the bottle but transferred to holding tanks for filtration, after which the wine is rebottled and the dosage added. Some wines produced by the transfer method bear the label "naturally fermented in the bottle."

Ullage—
the amount of wine lost during aging through evaporation or leakage.

Varietal—
the term applied to wines that contain at least 75 percent of the grape variety named on the label (e.g., Cabernet Sauvignon, Pinot Noir, Chardonnay); many vintners use a greater percentage in order to emphasize its characteristic flavor and aroma.

Veraison—
a stage in the growth of grapes when they begin to gain sugar and color levels; grapes change from green to purple in red varieties and to yellow or opaque green in white varieties.

Vertical tasting—
comparing consecutive vintages in a tasting.

Vin de Paille—
cutting techniques that allow grapes to dry in the sun.

Vintage date—
the year the grapes in a wine were harvested; a vintage date on the label indicates that at least 95 percent of the grapes are from that year.

Vintner—
the person who is involved in some way with the winemaking process of a winery, usually the owner.

Viticultural area—
see Appellation.

Viticulture—
the science and process of grape growing.

Vitis labrusca—
a hardy species of grapevine, including such varieties as Concord and Delaware, native to North America; used in winemaking in the eastern United States and Canada and as disease-resistant rootstock for *vinifera* vines.

Vitis vinifera—
the classic family of grapevines, including such premium grapes as Cabernet Sauvignon and Chardonnay, imported from Europe and particularly well-suited to the gentle climate of California.

Volatile—
excessive amounts of acid in wine.

White Riesling grape—
a white grape of German origin that is planted on more than 11,000 acres in California, as well as in Washington, Oregon and the east coast. It is used mainly for sweet white wines and may also be referred to as Johannisberg Riesling.

Wine thief—
a long glass tube used to extract samples of wine from the barrel.

Zinfandel grape—
the most common grape in California, where more than 27,000 acres are planted. It has gained popularity with the white and pink Zinfandels of late. It is believed to be the oldest variety, possibly imported from southern Italy by Count Agoston Haraszthy.

Wine Associations, Organizations and Information

WINE ASSOCIATIONS AND ORGANIZATIONS

Amador Vintners Association
P.O. Box 667, Plymouth, CA 95669.
(209) 245-6942; FAX (209) 245-6617.

American Vintners Association
1850 K St. N.W., #500, Washington,
D.C. 20006.
(800) 879-4637; FAX (202) 778-8087.

California North Coast Grape Growers
P.O. Box 213, Ukiah, CA 95482.
(707) 462-1361.

Carneros Quality Alliance
P.O. Box 178, Vineburg, CA 95487.
(707) 938-5906; FAX (707) 996-0145.

Central Coast Wine Growers Association
P.O. Box 14860, San Luis Obispo, CA
93406.
Phone and FAX (805) 534-9513.

Edna Valley & Arroyo Grande Valley Vintners Association
2195 Corbett Canyon Rd., Arroyo
Grande, CA 93420.
(805) 541-5868; FAX (805) 544-7205.

El Dorado Winery Association
2701 E St., Sacramento, CA 95816
(mailing address: P.O. Box 1614,
Placerville, CA 95667).
(916) 446-6562, (800) 306-3956;
FAX (916) 448-9115.

Lake County Grape Growers Association
65 Soda Bay Rd., Lakeport, CA 95453.
(707) 263-0911.

Livermore Valley Winegrower's Association
P.O. Box 2052, Livermore, CA
94551.
(510) 447-9463 (WINE).

Lodi Vintners Inc.
P.O. Box 1398, Woodbridge, CA
95258.
(209) 368-5338.

Mendocino County Vintners Association
P.O. Box 1409, Ukiah, CA 95482.
(707) 468-1343.

Monterey Wine Country Association
P.O. Box 1793, Monterey, CA 93942.
(408) 375-9400; FAX (408) 655-0354.

Napa Valley Grape Grower's Association
4075 Solano Ave., Napa, CA 94558-1793.
(707) 944-8311.

Napa Valley Vintners Association
P.O. Box 141, 900 Meadowood Ln., St. Helena, CA 94574.
(707) 963-0148.

The Organic Grapes into Wine Alliance
54 Genoa Pl., San Francisco, CA 94133.
(800) 477-0167.

Paso Robles Vintners and Growers
1940 Spring St., Paso Robles, CA 93446 (mailing address: P.O. Box 324, 93447).
(805) 239-8463 (VINE); FAX (805) 237-6439.

Russian River Wine Road Association
P.O. Box 46, Healdsburg, CA 95448.
(707) 433-6782, (800) 648-9922; FAX (707) 433-0237.

Santa Barbara County Vintners Association
P.O. Box 1558, Santa Ynez, CA 93460-1558.
(805) 688-0881, 686-5881.

Santa Clara Valley Wine Growers Association
P.O. Box 1192, Morgan Hill, CA 95037.

Santa Cruz Mountains Wine Growers Association
P. O. Box 3000, Santa Cruz, CA 95063.
(408) 479-WINE (9463); FAX (408) 688-6961.

Silverado Trail Wineries Association
P.O. Box 453, Deer Park, CA 94576.
(707) 586-0803; FAX (707) 257-3311.

Sonoma Counties Wineries Association
5000 Roberts Rd., Rohnert Park, CA 94928.
(707) 586-3795; FAX (707) 586-1383.

Sonoma Valley Vintners & Growers: An Appellation Alliance
453 First St. E., Sonoma, CA 95476.
(707) 935-0803; FAX (707) 996-9212.

Southern San Joaquin Valley Winegrape Growers Association
4358 Laval Rd., Arvin, CA 93202.
(805) 858-2291.

Temecula Valley Vintners Association
P.O. Box 1601, Temecula, CA 92593-1601.
(909) 699-3626.

Winegrowers of Dry Creek Valley
P.O. Box 1796, Healdsburg, CA 95448.
Phone and FAX (707) 433-3031.

WINE & VISITOR CENTERS

A Taste of Monterey Visitors Center
7100 Cannery Row, Monterey, CA 93940.
(408) 646-5446.

Los Olivos Wine & Spirits Emporium
P.O. Box 783, Los Olivos, CA 93441-0783.
(805) 688-4409; FAX (805) 687-1024.

Robert Mondavi Wine & Food Center
1570 Scenic Ave., Costa Mesa, CA 92626.
(714) 979-4510; FAX (714) 979-5616.

**Sonoma County Wine &
Visitors Center**
*5000 Roberts Rd., Rohnert Park, CA
94928.*
(707) 586-3795; FAX (707) 586-1383.

WINE EDUCATION

**The American Institute of
Wine & Food**
*1550 Bryant St., San Francisco, CA
94103.*
(415) 255-3000; FAX (415) 255-2874.

**American Society for Enology
and Viticulture**
P.O. Box 1855, Davis, CA 95617.
(916) 753-3142.

American Wine Society
3006 Latta Rd., Rochester, NY 14612.
Phone and FAX (716) 225-7613.

The National Wine Coalition
NWC newsletter, Wine Trends &
Perspectives
*1703 Rhode Island Ave. N.W. #402,
Washington, D.C. 20036.*
(202) 785-9510; FAX (202) 785-9402.

Society of Wine Educators
*132 Shaker Rd., East Longmeadow, MA
01028.*
(413) 567-8272.

Wine Appreciation Guild
*155 Connecticut, San Francisco, CA
94107.*
(800) 231-9463.

Wine Institute
*425 Market St., #1000, San Francisco,
CA 94105.*
(415) 851-2319.

Women for WineSense
P.O. Box 2098, Yountville, CA 94599.
(415) 851-2319.

PUBLICATIONS

California Visitors Review
P.O. Box 92, El Verano, CA 95433.
*(707) 938-0780, 938-3494
(subscriptions); FAX 938-3674.*
Single copy $2.50; annual $36.

This weekly black and white, newsprint
publication contains northern and central California winery and area information written for the visitor: dining, art
and antiques, shopping, bed and breakfast inns, lodging, attractions and events.

Napa Valley Appellation
P.O. Box 516, Napa, CA 94559.
(800) 799-22679 (subscriptions).
Single copy $3.50; annual $18.

Published bimonthly, this is a full-color
glossy magazine reflecting wine country
lifestyles in the Napa Valley wine
appellation; written for those living in,
or interested in, the Napa Valley region.

Wine Spectator
*P.O. Box 50462, Boulder, CO
80322-0462.*
(800) 752-7799 (subscriptions).
Single copy $2.95; annual $40.

This semimonthly, oversized full-color
magazine is written for the wine
consumer and contains profiles of
wineries and owners, winemakers, wine
reviews, buying guides and features and
industry news and information.

Wines & Vines
*1800 Lincoln Avenue, San Rafael, CA
94901-9930.*
*(415) 453-9700 (subscriptions); FAX
(415) 453-2517.*
Directory $45; annual $32.50.

Published for more than 75 years, this
monthly magazine contains the latest
news, trends, statistics, insights, trade
opinions and perspectives; considered
the best source for up-to-date information on all "insider" aspects of the industry; written for those in the wine industry.
Their annual directory and buyers guide
is known as the "industry Bible."

Index

Index to Advertisers

For information about placing and advertisement in Automobile Club of Southern California publications, please contact:

Karen Clyne or Ginger Nichols
Advertising Services H076
Auto Club of Southern California
P.O. Box 2890
Los Angeles, CA 90051
(213) 741-3571